The Idea of Great Poetry

The
Idea of Great Poetry
By Lascelles Abercrombie

Select Bibliographies Reprint Series

 BOOKS FOR LIBRARIES PRESS
FREEPORT, NEW YORK

First Published 1925
Reprinted 1969

STANDARD BOOK NUMBER:
8369-5083-6

LIBRARY OF CONGRESS CATALOG CARD NUMBER:
73-99654

PRINTED IN THE UNITED STATES OF AMERICA

CONTENTS

PREFACE

THESE lectures are meant to form a kind of sequel to two previous publications—"*An Essay towards a Theory of Art*" and "*The Theory of Poetry*." The methods and principles stated generally in the first book, and used to theorize the facts of a particular art in the second, are here carried a stage further, and made the argument of a specific line of criticism. Anything like a critical survey of the topic was, however, no part of my intention ; I merely wished to show how criticism, which assesses the merits of individual works, may derive authority from theory, which judges the nature and function of works of art as a class ; a purpose which would be facilitated by attending to one particular kind of merit—and the merit of "greatness" seemed to offer favourable scope for the continuation of theory into criticism. The argument, then, was my main concern; the criticism—obviously incomplete as a survey, even of the most cursory sort—being brought in merely to substantiate it.

When the Master of Trinity honoured me with an invitation to be Clark Lecturer in 1923, this was the topic I chose. The argument I then set out, along with a good deal of its critical illustration, is here reproduced ; but in a somewhat castigated form, as may be judged by the reduction of a dozen lectures to five. A short book is better than a long one. I gladly took an opportunity, offered in the following year by an invitation from Bangor, to recast my argument into closer connexion, and to condense the matter of its criticism. The Ballard Matthews Lectures which I was privileged to give last winter in the University College of North Wales are here printed almost as they were delivered.

L. A.

LECTURE I

DICTION AND EXPERIENCE. MOMENTS OF GREATNESS

§ 1

THE title of this course of lectures—*The Idea of Great Poetry*—sufficiently indicates its purpose. I do not, however, by any means intend to lay down *a priori* the qualities which I suppose poetry *ought* to have in order to deserve the epithet " great " ; my endeavour will simply be to enquire what *are* the qualities most noticeable in the poetry which has, as a matter of acknowledged fact, been recognized as great. I assume, you see, that great poetry is somehow recognizable; and I go on to ask what that recognition involves, and how it is made. Without that assumption, I could not, of course, begin to talk about great poetry at all. But that it is an assumption on which I can safely ground my argument seems tolerably clear from the habit of holding centenary celebrations, which has

7

The Idea of Great Poetry

lately been growing on us. These outbursts of praise in accordance with the calendar, this dutiful connexion of enthusiasm with multiples of a hundred, may look a little factitious. But the habit at any rate shows how unmistakeable, in the long run, the great poet becomes. We have lately taken centenary occasions to celebrate the greatness of Shakespeare, Dante, Keats, Shelley and Byron; we have busied ourselves, if not on our own account, then vicariously in the newspapers, with the appreciation of these poets in their several qualities. Would it not be useful if, from this centenary habit of ours, we proceeded to ask ourselves, What exactly do we mean by a great poet? How, when we call Dante and Shakespeare great poets, do their remarkable differences come to be classified under one title? And what are we relying on, when we call Shelley a great poet, but not so great as Shakespeare? Suppose the almanac had been even kinder, and had added to our list other names equally convincing—such names as Homer, Milton Goethe, to say nothing of Leopardi and Heine, Sophocles and Racine. What sort of similarity can

Diction and Experience

it be, which the world perceives in such a miscellany of talents and achievements ? But if we can make this similarity out, would it not improve our understanding, and therefore our enjoyment, of these talents and achievements—not only by appreciating their common function, but in the result sharpening also thereby our sense of their individual qualities ?

There are those, I know, who deny that greatness has, properly speaking, anything to do with poetry. These are the sticklers for what, by a rather noticeable begging of the question, they call *pure poetry*. If a poem is the essence of what a poem should be (they make themselves the judges of that, of course), if a poem is as good as it can be, they say, what else matters ? Perfection is what we are to look for ; the scale of the achievement bears no relation to its *poetic* success. If it is strictly a question of poetry and of nothing else, why must we prefer Shakespeare's plays to his songs ? This concern with greatness—what is it but obedience to a mere vulgar prejudice ?

Well, let it be that. *Homo sum :* this vulgar

The Idea of Great Poetry

prejudice, then, is my topic. It is a prejudice, at any rate, of some standing ; the idea of greatness in literature is as old as criticism itself. It is no better for that, says our objector ; is there to be no progress in our criticism, as in our other activities ?—Let us hope so ; but leaving on one side the question, what progress in criticism is, we may on our part ask, is there any reason why new notions should necessarily be better than old ? *Change* is inevitable, no doubt, here as elsewhere ; but it may sometimes be more profitable to change by re-stating old opinion rather than by replacing it with new. I think that must be the case here ; for it can hardly be mere coincidence, that those who profess themselves superior to the notion of greatness in poetry, should be so markedly less interesting, in themselves and in all their habits and customs, than the poets and critics who accept it.

But I shall have enough to do without prescribing for that peculiar eyesight to which all stars are of the same magnitude. Who supposes that all poetry, even all the poetry which is to be called

Diction and Experience

supremely good, must have all possible qualities ? We may easily agree that poetic success as such is independent of scale. Poetry may certainly be supremely good without being great ; though I cannot conceive how it should be great poetry without also being good poetry. But there is in certain poems a quality which is recognized by common consent as *greatness*. I call it a quality ; it may turn out to be a peculiar combination of qualities. But that makes no difference ; it is then a quality of their qualities. Well, it is just this common consent, and the grounds of it, that I wish to investigate. But note that scale is certainly not the crucial thing even here. A long poem may as easily miss being great as a poem of molecular size—the smallest poem which can exist as such. Can a short poem, however, possess the quality of greatness ? That is one of the questions we are to investigate ; always remembering that a poem may be inestimably precious for other things besides greatness.

But I ought not to leave this modern notion of *pure poetry* without examining a little further its

The Idea of Great Poetry

supposed power of damaging the old idea of *great poetry*. I have seen it argued that when Homer or Dante or Shakespeare is praised for the greatness of his poetry, it is not really the poetry that is being praised, but the man. And, though this kind of reasoning implies an intolerable and quite artificial limitation of the idea of poetry, there may be some excuse for it. Too often the poetry which is accepted as great has been praised for its ideas, its passions, its characterization, without any appreciable regard for the conditions which enable these (or any other) qualities to exist *as poetry*. We are invited to admire them as if it were a matter of indifference, that they are elements in a work of art. What does that mean ? It means, ultimately, that they have the importance, not necessarily of logical, moral, or practical validity, but simply of notable experience —the immediate interest of experience which cannot be entered without delighted excitement of intellect, emotion, or imagination, and which need not justify itself outside that excitement : its validity is self-evident : it is its own standard. And, in the art which we are now considering,

Diction and Experience

we can only be urged to enter into such experience by the provocations of language wrought up to a consummate force and nicety of expressiveness.

Yet it is quite easy to see why this should come to be ignored, in many analyses of the greatness of poetry. It is not the magic of language itself which accounts for greatness, but that which comes to us through and by means of magical language. Nevertheless, to ignore this means is to leave out the characteristic fact, the fact that it is *poetry* we are dealing with. The omission is, accordingly, protested ; and the pendulum swings right across to the notion that magical language is the only thing that matters. But no one can stop there. Language can only be magical when there is a purpose in its magic. No sort of language can exist for its own sake. But when is its magic most apparent ? Clearly, when what is effected cannot possibly be distinguished from what is effecting it : all we can do is to acknowledge the enchantment. This, then, will be *pure poetry ;* as thus :

The Idea of Great Poetry

Come unto these yellow sands
  And then take hands,
Curtsied when you have and kist
  The wild waves whist.
Foot it featly here and there
  And sweet sprites bear
The burthen—Hark !—(Bow-wow !)
The watch-dogs bark !—(Bow-wow !)
Hark, hark I hear
The strain of strutting chanticleer
Cry cock-a-diddle-dow.

But if you have to search appreciably beyond the skill of the language in order to find its final purpose, if you have to go to ideas, passions, characters, significances, which can be distinguisht and discussed apart from the language which pointed you to them, then (they say) you are dealing with adulterated poetry, with poetry which has admitted some mixture of what is alien to its own peculiar magic ; and if great poetry takes you in this direction, then it takes you *away* from the essential nature of poetry. Poetry only preserves its purity so long as it resides in those prime immediacies of sense, feeling, imagination, which, once poetry

Diction and Experience

has *said* them, leave us nothing to say *about* them.

That is the argument ; and there is nothing wrong with it except that by *poetry* it means *lyrical poetry*. One may perhaps prefer lyrical poetry to all other kinds ; but the didactic heresy itself was not more arbitrary or illogical than the attempt to confine the scope of poetry within its lyrical effort. Who disputes that poetry, to be supreme in its own nature, must be pure and unadulterated ? But what is pure poetry ? What but the poetry which expresses pure experience ? And that simply means— *experience itself :* experience valued merely as such, in and for itself, without having to rely on any external judgement of truth or morality or utility. The flowering of a cherry-tree, the dancing of a child, the attitude of a mountain, the sound and motion of waves, the sense of youth and love and mortality—we all know how these, and the like of these, dispense with any ulterior judgement, and give us the momentary, unconsidered rapture of *pure experience*. But where are its boundaries ? There are none. Nothing whatever which the

15

The Idea of Great Poetry

human spirit is capable of receiving, is incapable of being received simply as a pure experience, valued without needing any verdict of an ulterior judgement, appreciable simply as a particle of active life. And the really characteristic thing about the art of poetry is its power to present the whole conceivable world—the world not merely of sense and fantasy, but of severest intellectual effort, of subtlest psychological understanding, of the highest ardors of mutinous or consenting passion—to present anything which any faculty of ours can achieve or accept, as a moment of mere delighted living, of self-sufficient experience.

So now, after these preliminaries, I begin my attempt to build up roughly, but as substantially as I can, the *idea of great poetry*. I mean to imitate in my building the most elementary of architectural forms, the pyramid. I shall take first, as the broad foundation, squaring them to the purpose of the whole design, those obvious and necessary qualities which *all* poetry must have ; and successively impose on these the qualities which, in this particular valuation of *greatness*, raise poetry higher and higher—but which occur more and more rarely—until at last we reach the narrow apex, the qualities of supreme greatness.

Of course, when we discuss poetry quality by quality, we are proceeding more in accordance with convenience than with truth. Poetry does not consist of separable qualities ; if it exists at all, it exists as an indivisible whole. Unless, however, we were to allow ourselves, here as elsewhere in life, the liberty of analysing, criticism could never get much farther than exclamations of " well done ! " and " ill done ! " The disadvantage is, however, that when we come to the superstructure of our argument, we may seem to be ignoring the fundamental qualities on which it necessarily rests. I hope it will be allowed, during the later stages of our discussion, that nothing which is there said to make for *greatness* has been admitted except under the conditions which make it *poetry*, though these conditions may not be expressly mentioned : for they will, in fact, have been mentioned once and for all as the foundations of everything else.

The Idea of Great Poetry

What, then, is the first thing which we require of all poetry—not merely in order to be great, but to exist at all ? It has already been indicated. I will call it, compendiously, " incantation " : the power of using words so as to produce in us a sort of enchantment ; and by that I mean a power not merely to charm and delight, but to kindle our minds into unusual vitality, exquisitely aware both of things and of the connexions of things. This, of course, cannot be taken as a detachable crafts-manship ; try to do so and, like chipping varnish off woodwork, it flies to pieces : we can make nothing of it. Nevertheless, the exceptional way words in poetry will command our minds is the first thing criticism can lay hold of : the first thing we come to know distinctly, as soon as we begin to study our delight. We do not require an absolute enchantment in every phrase we read, even in the finest poetry. The poets have an art of making us expect the magical phrase ; and when it comes, it casts its enchantment over the whole surrounding

18

Diction and Experience

texture of language. But unless it does come, and come often enough to keep our minds invigorated by its release, even from common words, of uncommon energy of meaning, we begin to murmur : " This may be very sincere and painstaking, but it is not *poetry*."

When Theseus, in *The Knight's Tale*, cuts down a whole wood for a funeral pyre, Chaucer disclaims, very minutely, any intention to describe the business. And no wonder ! Who wants description when he can have incantation ? Every detail, which Chaucer mentions as something he will not describe, is mentioned in such magical words that it flashes out at us like the light of a diamond. Let a single instance suffice. The dense wood has been all cut down, and the havoc cleared away ; and Chaucer says he will not tell us how the nymphs and the fauns, the beasts and the birds, fled away in fear :

Ne how the ground agast was of the light.

Well might he disclaim *description !* And if we wish to account to ourselves our delighted astonishment in that line, surely the first thing we should lay hold of would be the astonishing and delightful efficacy of that one word *agast*. Why, with that word, the line becomes such an incantation, that we feel what the very ground itself was feeling : the ground has become alive and sentient in our minds. Words have not *described* a fact, they have re-created in our minds the very fact itself.

Where was this fact originally ? In Chaucer's mind : but he found the words which could transfer, perfect and unimpaired, this piece of his mind into ours. So did Herrick, when his gliding Julia passed, sumptuously languishing, before his admiration :

> Whenas in silks my Julia goes,
> Then, then (me thinks) how sweetly flows
> That liquefaction of her clothes.

Herrick's Julia, after that, is everyone's Julia. And it is not Herrick *describing* what he loves to admire : our minds have become a moment of Herrick himself, admiring and making harmless love. As with Herrick and his Julia, so with Casca and his lion : it is a unique moment of life that enters our minds

Diction and Experience

when Casca tells us how, during the night of prodigies in Rome, he met the lion,

> Who glazed upon me and went surly by.

There was never any other lion quite like that. And the sight of its mysterious demeanour has been made over to us in perpetuity. The very sense of Casca's appalled encounter is absolute in us; Shakespeare's art has so enchanted us, that we become, for a moment, what he became.

There are, naturally, infinite occasions for the poet's incantation; but its purpose is always the same. It may be giving us simply a moment of sensation: but it will make the moment individual, exquisite, unique. If I told you I had seen a scatter of rose leaves floating on water, you might guess the sight had pleased me; and you would no doubt call up in your minds some vision fairly corresponding with mine. But when the poet writes:

> And on the water, *like to burning coals*
> *On liquid silver*, leaves of roses lay:

it is a quite special vision of floating rose leaves that is imposed on us. Such delicate extravagance

The Idea of Great Poetry

of diction gives a personal distinction to the image ; and chiefly by distinctly charging it with the poet's vivid and singular delight. The distinction of the moment will, no doubt, be even more noticeable, if the sensation comes to us not merely alive with appropriate feeling, but complicated with some unusual peculiarity of mood and allusion : something quaint and fantastic, perhaps, as when the same poet—Giles Fletcher—sees the first light of dawn strike the pines on the mountain-side, and says of it that the trees

> Dandled the morning's childhood in their arms.

Or it may be something remote and mysterious, like the obscure sympathy which Keats divined in the very stones of his landscape, when

> Crag jutting forth to crag, and rocks that seemed
> Ever as if just rising from a sleep,
> Forehead to forehead held their monstrous horns.

Whatever it be, the poet's words not only make the whole fact start alive in our minds ; they are electric with the subtle distinction of the moment in which the fact occurs, stored with those delicate

Diction and Experience

and profound reverberations which make the fact unique. For the facts we are speaking of are experiences ; and experiences are always unique : they occur in some particular person's mind, in some particular sequence of other experiences. Now poetry is the translation of experience into language ; and the translation has not properly been made at all, unless, along with the stuff of the experience, goes a rendering of its peculiar moment, instinct with the moods, implications, references, influences, which made the moment unique. My instances have been mainly visual—whether actual or imaginary makes, of course, no difference. But whatever the nature of his topic, the poet's business is always the same. He must, out of the subtly adjusted sound and sense of words, contrive such a texture of intensities and complexities of meaning, of unsuspected filaments of fine allusion and suggestion, as will enable these gossamers to capture and convey into our minds just those fleeting, gleaming qualities of experience which elude the hold of every-day straightforward language. For these are the very qualities which give to each moment of

23

The Idea of Great Poetry

experience its unique distinction ; and the words that can securely convey them are magical words, for they are truly creative. They have that incantation in them which can create in us, over and over again, the complete and many-coloured sense of a notably individual experience : the poet's experience. It is, indeed, *our* sense of it ; and in becoming our sense of it, it no doubt undergoes inevitable modulation. But that does not lessen its individuality as an experience.

I have been speaking so far of the momentary phrases of enchantment : the phrases on which the spirits of imagination assemble as incalculably as the scholastic angels on the point of a needle. But when poetry is a continuous creation in us of the poet's habit of mind and its peculiar commerce with the world, then that poet, we say, has achieved *style :* that is, *his own* style, the habit of language nicely corresponding with the characteristic mode of his life. In any case, the magical infection of our minds with the poet's mind by means of language, is the first thing poetry must be capable of, in order to exist at all ; and to accept the incantation—the

Diction and Experience

re-creation in us of another man's experience,—is to make our first acknowledgement of the presence of poetry. I do not mean, however, by adopting this use of the word " magical " (common enough nowadays), to suggest that poets do not know very well what they are about, and just how to effect it.

Poetry is an art singularly privileged. It penetrates deeper, and mixes more intimately into our lives, than any other art, because the vehicle of its power is language ; and language is the very faculty of spiritual existence in this world, as well as the means whereby human ability transacts its affairs. But poetry has to pay for its privilege. Men exist in nations ; and the affairs of no nation can be quite like the affairs of another. Poetry is the most local of the arts. Dante, as is well known, scornfully refused to expound his poetry to " Tedeschi e Inglesi," to whom, he says, his art could never reveal its beauty. And he went on to utter his solemn protest against its translation :

E però sappia ciascuno, che nulla cosa per legame musaico armonizzata si può della sua loquela in altra trasmutare, senza rompere tutta sua dolcezza e armonia.

The Idea of Great Poetry

There is no disputing this judgement. You cannot carry the fine interactions of the words of one language over into another ; and this means, that you cannot transfer from one language to another the nice individuality of the poet's experience : the very thing, namely, that gave to his words the status of poetry. The moment which his language has exquisitely distinguisht is likely to become, in a translation, common and unnoticeable. Such lines as these may seem nothing extraordinary in their diction ; but try to translate them, and see what happens :

ὑμεῖς δ'ἃ φράζω δρᾶτε, καὶ τάχ' ἄν μ' ἴσως
πύθοισθε κεἰ νῦν δυστυχῶ σεσωσμένον. . . .

denique tanto opere in dubiis trepidare periclis
quae mala nos subigit vitai tanta cupido. . . .

a questa tanto picciola vigilia
de' nostri sensi ch' è del rimanente,
non vogliate negar l'esperienza. . . .

The best that can happen is that the translator may be poet enough to provide out of his own life and art some substitute for what has vanisht. How splendidly this may happen, let the Authorized

26

Diction and Experience

Version of *Job* or *The Wisdom of Solomon* remind
us ; but the result will be, in effect, a new poem.
Sometimes, indeed, in what is called a translation,
the original has been the mere stimulus of a wholly
new creation : the famous instance is Fitzgerald's
Omar Khayyám. What is most likely to happen
is, however, that the translation will be not merely
out of the original language, but altogether out
of existence as poetry.

Yet something may survive, in either case : in
diminisht efficacy perhaps, or perhaps not as poetry
at all. And of all qualities, the quality of greatness
is most likely to survive somehow. Let Dante
witness against himself. No poet ever made words
mean so much ; no poet ever made language the
means of such distinction and intensity of individual
experience. In any translation, *The Divine Comedy*
must seem, moment by moment, to have suffered
an intolerable loss ; and yet the greatness of the
whole will substantially survive. And so, too, when
the translator substitutes for the original a poetic
craftsmanship peculiarly his own. Chapman's Homer
is quite unlike Pope's, and neither Chapman's nor

The Idea of Great Poetry

Pope's Homer is like Homer himself. Yet unmistakeably the greatness of both Chapman and Pope is Homer's greatness : this, in either paraphrase, is the surviving thing.

It would come in plausibly here, to object that, if greatness can survive the loss of poetry or a change of poetry, it can be no necessary or original part of poetry. But this would imply a thorough misconception of poetry's nature. Poetry exists as the perfect expression of experience, within the possibilities of language. In translation, the perfection of the expression is likely to go, because there is no exact equivalent of one language in another. The living reality can never be transported out of its native language ; but a serviceable indication of the living reality may nevertheless survive. It will be crippled, diminisht, truncated : an experience vainly demanding to live in the words of the man who experienced it, since only he can know what words will enable it to live completely and happily. But the nature of the experience may be plain enough, nevertheless ; even though it be degraded to the mere topic of the experience. It may be not only

28

Diction and Experience

plain, but still alive. If you are not a traveller, you may see in a menagerie the sort of beasts that live in foreign lands. You do not see them there living their ordained and distinctive lives ; for they are abstract beasts, remote from their native reality: they are, in fact, translations of beasts, and woefully incomplete. But they are still alive. Or, if you go to a museum, you may see the same beasts even more brutally translated. But as well say that tigers are no necessary part of tigers' lives, because the mere beasts themselves can be seen caged or stuft a thousand miles from India, as say that the greatness which can survive translation is shown thereby to be no necessary part of poetry. Whatever poetry has to express is a necessary part of it ; for it is by virtue of expressing this that it exists at all. The common mistake in these matters is the confusion of experience itself with the matter of experience. Poetry differs from the rest of literature precisely in this : it does not merely tell us *what* a man experienced, it makes his very experience itself live again in our minds ; by means of what I have called the incantation of its words. If you want to live in Dante's experience, Dante himself, in his own language, is the only person you can go to. But any decently competent translator can tell you *what* Dante experienced. He can never, however, tell you this completely or quite satisfactorily ; because the matter of an experience is nothing but an abstract of reality—of the experience itself.

This question of translation has not taken us into a digression which is wholly without bearing on our present purpose. Our concern is, to discuss the quality of those experiences which give greatness to the poetry designed to express them. Now, if *poetry's* greatness could not survive translation, still less would it be *poetry's* greatness which would be capable of discussion : for that must require a much more complete abstraction from its original existence. It can only be usefully discussed as something which did exist as poetic art ; but obviously, the greatness (or any other quality) of poetry will not be the same thing in discussion as it was in the art which prompted the discussion. The most conspicuous difference will be, that it is a less satisfactory thing : criticism is even more

Diction and Experience

like a museum than a menagerie. But the fact that
the animal on view there may be subjected to all
sorts of methodical comparisons and examinations,
and placed in a sedate series of resembling animals,
does not affect the fact that it was once a live animal.
Indeed, it is only in order to improve our under-
standing of the live animal, and its peculiar activities,
that we study our dead preparations of its species
at all.[1] And the museum of criticism has this
advantage, that its doors are always open, and
immediately outside them is wild country, full of
the living creatures that are but preserved specimens
within-doors. In a word, the living experience we

[1] By " a species of poem " is sometimes meant what would
be better and more simply called a *kind* of poem—lyric, epic,
elegy, satire, etc. : rough distinctions which have no validity
except occasional convenience. It is, however, in quite strict
analogy with biological classification to call any particular poem
—*The Divine Comedy*, or *Paradise Lost*, for example—a species :
a species made up of an indefinite number of variable indi-
viduals. A poem exists as an individual in the mind of each
person who reads it ; but in its possibility of multiplying these
individual existences without losing in their variation a consistent
and characteristic uniformity, it exists as a species ; and it is
as a species that we usually refer to it.

have had in poetry becomes in criticism the mere matter of experience. That is a remarkable difference, never to be forgotten : and I am wholly in agreement with anyone who says, that it is not only a difference, but a degradation, as plainly as the museum-specimen is a degradation of the divinely alive beast. But only so can we take accurate account of our experience ; and perhaps the accurate man is the only kind of man whose existence is excusable. The thing is, that we can, in our topic, pass at once from the account of experience back to the living experience itself ; and if our account has indeed been accurate, in depth as well as in breadth, we go back to an experience which we find has enormously enricht and invigorated itself. That, at least, is the apology for studies such as these.

§ 3

But why should we delight in other people's experience ? For if we delight in poetry, that is what it comes to. Have we not enough life of our own, that we should go to the poet for his ? Indeed, no ; we can never have enough : especially we can

never have enough of the life that is most truly
alive—intensely and delightedly conscious of itself,
exulting in its faculties and in the world which calls
them into use. We certainly do not need for this
any uncommon or astonishing matter. Some of the
most captivating moments in poetry are precisely
those that render the most ordinary things. When
Cowper takes his early morning walk in winter,
surely the incident that must please us most is the
sight he catches of his own shadow. The " slanting
ray " of the sun, he says,

> Slides ineffectual down the snowy vale
> And, tinging all with his own rosy hue,
> From every herb and every spiry blade
> Stretches a length of shadow o'er the field.
> Mine, spindling into longitude immense,
> In spite of gravity, and sage remark
> That I myself am but a fleeting shade,
> Provokes me to a smile. With eye askance
> I view the muscular proportioned limb
> Transformed to a lean shank. The shapeless pair,
> As they designed to mock me, at my side
> Take step for step ; and as I near approach
> The cottage, walk along the plastered wall,
> Preposterous sight ! the legs without the man.

C

The Idea of Great Poetry

There is no occasion for any conspicuous verbal magic here; but there is enough to make the incident alive. And what a pleasant incident it is, the sight we catch of our legs (for Cowper's legs as we read become our legs) thus parodied beside us on the bright ground, absurdly opening and shutting like a crazy pair of scissors, and then surprisingly jerking upright on the cottage wall, " the legs without the man ! "

And yet, does it need a poet to give us an experience so simple as this ; so trivial, one might think, as to be hardly worth noticing ? But that is it : nothing is beneath a poet's notice. What pleases us here is the thing that pleases us (and a good deal more than pleases) in every experience that poetry can invest us with : not so much the substance of the experience, whether commonplace or farfetched, as the quality of it. The poet (assuming that he is justifying his title) has been as keenly alive to it as if it was the novelty of the world. Let it be the order of the stars in heaven, or the shadow of his legs on the ground : whatever, when he is indeed a poet, catches his attention, catches

Diction and Experience

it entire and engages his whole spirit in the experience of it. It is in this sense that the experience capable of producing poetry is something extraordinary : in that it is an experience on which a whole personality has been focussed with peculiar intensity and delight : experience, we may say, exceptionally conscious of itself. Poetry, we often hear, is ideal life : and so it is, as I shall, later on, have to argue more largely. But poetry does not need to decline the actual in order to be ideal ; it is ideal in the *manner* of its experience—an image of the ideal way of experiencing this present world of here and now.

Well, this is true of poetry in general. How much nearer has it brought us to the idea of great poetry ? Here I must return to my original assumption—the assumption that great poetry is *recognizable ;* for, once more, my only purpose is to enquire what the world means when it calls this or that poetry *great.* But to make our recognition secure, we must set up some sort of contrast. Read, for example, *The Knotting Song*, by Sir Charles Sedley :

The Idea of Great Poetry

Hears not my Phillis how the birds
 Their feathered mates salute ?
They tell their passion in their words :
 Must I alone be mute ?
  Phillis, without frown or smile,
  Sat and knotted all the while. . . .

And so on ! A delicious moment ! And is there
not an exquisitely personal distinction in it ? And
could anything be better as art than the precision
and proportion of its rendering into language ? But
no one would suggest that Sedley's version of
unpropitious love has anything of the quality we
call greatness. Contrast it with the half dozen lines
with which Swinburne evokes the spirit of Sappho.
After Sedley, there may seem a suspicion of rant,
but there is surely the accent of greatness, in the
torrent of simile and metaphor that throngs into
the passion of Swinburne's imagination :

The intolerable infinite desire
Made my face pale like faded fire
 When the ashen pyre falls through with heat.
My blood was hot wan wine of love,
And my song's sound the sound thereof,
 The sound of the delight of it.

36

Diction and Experience

" Why," you may say, " the difference is already accounted for, when you admit that there is *passion* here. Sedley's elegance makes no pretence of passion ; but Swinburne's vehemence exists for nothing else. Why look further ? " But we must look further : for this really tells us very little about what we are trying to find. You cannot make out that greatness in poetry always depends on this sort of passion. Besides, what exactly is passion ? And why should it make poetry great ? For note that poetry cannot give a passion direct ; we can only get it indirectly, from the imagery that embodies it. Is it the kind of the imagery, or its extent, or its complexity, or what, that gives us a sense of greatness ?

We must, at any rate, try to find, in our sense of such a difference as that between Sedley and Swinburne, something broad enough to account generally for the accent of greatness : for the fact which we are investigating is just this—that extraordinarily divergent instances of poetry may all deserve the epithet " great." How do they come to deserve it ? Clearly, there must be something common to them all ; and clearly the value of it cannot be discussed until we have decided what it is.

After Swinburne's Sappho, let us contrast Sedley with Sappho herself. Certainly, the full sense of her greatness can only be given in her own magical language ; the impossibility of rendering the many-coloured splendor of her diction is notorious. But even in the blurr of a translation, there survives unmistakeably the character of that for which the incantation of her language was designed. The unknown incomparable critic, to whom we owe the preservation of *The Ode to Anactoria*, said that it was not so much a passion as a concourse of passions. This is often quoted ; and the keen insight of that phrase, " a concourse of passions," brings us near to what we are looking for. But the critic had more than this to say. It was not only the concourse of *passions* which he noticed ; it is a marvel, he says, how Sappho fuses together " soul, body, ears, tongue, eyes, colour. Uniting contradictions, she is, at one and the same time, hot and cold, in her senses and out of her mind, fearfully alive and

Diction and Experience

almost dead." And he completes his brilliant analysis by adding the essential thing : the singular excellence of this poetry, he says, is that all these form in it " a combination into a single whole."[1]

Now here we have got to something broader and deeper than the mere existence of passion in a poem. This puts poetic greatness on universal ground. Poetry is always the communication of unusually vivid experience, charged with an unusually personal delight. The sense of the greatness of poetry is nothing but a sense of the *richness* of each moment of the life which is being communicated to us. But we must note carefully what this implies. Momentary richness of experience means also an intensity of experience. It will not be a richness that runs

[1] He does not mean the " single whole " of the complete poem : the phrase (ἡ εἰς ταὐτὸ συναίρεσις) simply refers to the fusion of all these passions and sensations into a single momentary complex of experience. Accordingly, he quotes, not the whole poem, but just enough of it to show this. Unfortunately, therefore, the whole poem no longer exists, and we can only illustrate from it the greatness that exists in notable moments.

out in diffusion nor one that is amassed in confusion : it will come out of a life the conscious vigor of which may in any single moment be sensuous, emotional and intellectual all at once ; all distinctly imagined, along with their fine radiations of significance and allusion, yet all combined in an inextricable harmony. That is why I emphasize the *personal* quality of poetic experience, in the elucidation of its greatness. For only a life centred in a white heat of exultant personality and power of self-knowledge *could* accept and fuse into single moments of experience—into single intuitions—the infinite wealth offered to it by the occasions of great poetry, lavisht on it by every faculty of sense and mind and spirit. That which any one moment of great poetry concentrates into its harmony would, in ordinary experience, be dispersed through a whole series of moments. And this is why the language of great poetry must always be notable for its enchantment, for its power of collecting many kinds of meaning round a single phrase ; yet this richness and intensity of experience explains also why even a prose trans-

Diction and Experience

lation of great poetry will be worth reading : however much is lost, there is still more that must survive.

Now how do we stand as regards our contrast with Sedley ? Taking them simply as versions of experience, *The Knotting Song* and *The Ode to Anactoria* may be equally successful. We praise the intensity of Sappho's art ; but the mood which Sedley's delicate nicety of art renders so perfectly has all the intensity it will bear. We praise the splendor of Sappho's diction ; but Sedley's is just as exquisitely adequate to its occasion. The thing simply is, that there was incomparably more in any moment of Sappho's experience than in any moment of Sedley's. In any moment, therefore, her life had to collect itself into a far brighter and more ardent intensity of focus than his ; the command of her personality must immeasurably transcend his. But, as far as adequacy of art is concerned, we must not say that Sedley is below Sappho ; we should rather say that, in order to be as adequate as Sedley's, Sappho's art was bound, moment by moment, to achieve beyond any comparison a keener

and fuller expressiveness, a more magical incanta-
tion, than his.

This is what we mean, and all we mean, when
we call *The Ode to Anactoria* greater poetry than
The Knotting Song. To make it still clearer, let me
bring in another though similar contrast with the
latter : an early ode of Dante's, written in his
unregenerate days, and certainly one of the greatest
of his lyrics. Passion is still the theme ; and passion
disappointed—nay, enraged. But the passion is so
richly and solidly substantiated, that even a bare
summary of the poem may convey some notion
of its greatness. After preluding about his scornful
lady's impenetrable mood—her mind is as hard
and as cold as jasper, he says—all she has made
him suffer starts up before him into the towering
presence of a vision : he sees the armed Spirit of
Love striding terribly and triumphantly over him—
Love imagined as a malignant god exulting in
cruelty. He has been thrown to the ground, and
he feels himself there in bodily prostration under
the threat of that blinding sword ; the stroke
descends and pierces him, and he can but lie there

motionless, so tired with agony that his limbs are incapable even of shuddering. But while he is lying there, helplessly gazing up at that pitiless spirit, even then he is, in the very midst of his terrified anguish, feasting his imagination on the vengeance he will take on his lady for all his sufferings ; and first he is gleefully revenging himself on the detested beauty of her hair.

All this is given to us in that strain of impassioned intensity and majestic grace

> That bloom'd to immortalize the Tuscan style.

The perfection of Dante's diction here is one of the marvels of poetic art ; but merely to give you, as I have done, an abstract of the poem—and an incomplete abstract at that—is enough to indicate, past mistake, the nature of its greatness. For at the climax of the poem, consider what a throng of feeling and sensation has been poured by Dante's imagination into a single moment of consciousness. He feels the posture of his agonized fear, prone on the ground, frozen there in immoveable rigor ; he sees the dreadful face of the god blazing malignity at him, and the sword in act to strike ; and still, right at the heart of his agony, burns his own confident hope of revenge, already calculating its delight, intent on his mistress' hated loveliness, relishing the cruelty and lust he promises himself. That all this should be experienced in a lucid and coherent harmony of distinguishable elements is obviously the work of an astounding power of self-knowledge and organized self-command ; and Dante's supremely capable art transmits this faculty to us. Only in an exceptional intensity of conscious living, of active personality, could such a complex of riches make up a single moment of experience ; and, by virtue of the enchantment of language, this personal mastery of an infinite wealth has become our possession too, and everyone's.

Here we have, I cannot but believe, the general characteristic of all the poetry which strikes us as *great* : not only of that which is, as we say, subjective, but of the greatness of dramatic, narrative, reflective poetry also. The differentia is evidently one of degree only, but it is decisively noticeable. What we recognize in great poetry is this unconfused

Diction and Experience

complexity of rich experience, this confluence of all kinds of life into a single flame of consciousness, triumphantly asserting its luminous unity over all the manifold powers of its world. With Dante still in my mind, I take, to illustrate my theme further, and in objective substance, the first incident that occurs to me when I think of *The Divine Comedy* : an incident the more to my purpose for being so well known. The superb Farinata, as Dante approaches him, lifts himself erect out of his agony among the damned, " as though he had hell in great scorn " ; and abruptly and contemptuously greets the poet with the question, " Who were thy ancestors ? " At Dante's answer, he raises his eyebrows a little and says, " They were my fierce adversaries, and I broke them twice." And what a compound of the immortal grandeur and folly of human pride lives before us there ! It is in this sort of life, in this concentrated wealth of simultaneous impression, with its allusion all round to all sorts of experience, that we move continually throughout *The Divine Comedy*.

And note, that it is not merely the rich vitality

of the incident which gives us the sense of greatness, but the harmony which fuses the wealth of matter into a single compound of impression. That is the characteristic thing everywhere in *The Divine Comedy*; and is it not, as far as our recognition of greatness is concerned, the characteristic thing also throughout the *Iliad*? Take one instance only. Hector hurrying out to battle in radiant armour meets Andromache and the nurse, with his baby in her arms. Andromache sees the inevitable end—Hector killed, herself in abominable slavery. Hector sees it too ; better even than Andromache, he knows what the Greeks will do to her. But not even that anguish can weaken him. If these things must be, what can we do but endure them—nay, go out erect to meet them ? Then Hector reaches out his arms to his little boy to kiss him good-bye ; and the baby is frightened at his helmet, and cries. And we instantly realize that Hector, the man-slaying terror of the Greeks, is a Hector the baby has never seen before ; he has only known the daddy that played with him in the nursery. So Hector takes off his helmet and sets it gleaming on the ground :

Diction and Experience

and then the boy will come to him and be kissed. And Hector goes out to fight, and to accept his fate. And Andromache goes home, to await hers. Homer has there sublimed and compacted into a single living moment the whole lamentable infinite splendor of man's *courage*.

And exactly similar is the recognition of greatness when the power of imagination neither concentrates inwards on itself, nor dramatizes itself outwards in action, but meditates. When Shakespeare's petulant Achilles asks, " What, are my deeds forgot ? "— his Ulysses has an answer for him which is one of the greatest things in the world. Yet it could all be reduced to the merest commonplaces of proverbial wisdom. But this worldly lore has come to new and individual life in Shakespeare's mind ; it is being experienced there like a keenly appreciated event. It is something vividly happening, and all the powers of imagination come trooping together to join in. Common sense, without ceasing to be thought, turns also to a pomp of things seen and felt ; and the language of the poet gives us a rich and instantaneous harmony of imaginative experi-

ence which is thought, sensation, and feeling all
at once :

> Time hath, my lord, a wallet at his back
> Wherein he puts alms for oblivion,
> A great-sized monster of ingratitudes :
> Those scraps are good deeds past,
> Which are devour'd as fast as they are made,
> Forgot as soon as done : perseverance, dear my lord,
> Keeps honor bright : to have done, is to hang
> Quite out of fashion, like a rusty mail
> In monumental mockery.   Take the instant way ;
> For honor travels in a strait so narrow
> Where one but goes abreast ; keep then the path ;
> For emulation hath a thousand sons
> That one by one pursue : if you give way
> Or hedge aside from the direct forthright,
> Like to an enter'd tide they all rush by
> And leave you hindmost :
> Or, like a gallant horse fall'n in first rank,
> Lie there for pavement to the abject rear,
> O'er-run and trampled on. . . .

§ 4

But the greatness of this kind of poetry, you may
tell me, is due to the fact that it is distinctively and
specifically *imaginative :* its matter could not have
been presented at all, except by a lofty act of

Diction and Experience

symbolic imagination. For what is the real matter of this passage? Certainly not the *thought*; which, in itself, is nothing remarkable. But as it is represented to us in the poetry, in the noble procession of these images, it is singularly remarkable. Why? Because it is not presented to us simply as *thought*, but as the finely emotional and subtly allusive experience of an individual mind *thinking*—of, precisely, Shakespeare's Ulysses thinking. Only an exceptional power of capturing the intangible could have so exactly, so splendidly, given shape and feature to such fleeting significances: and there is no other power that can do this but an exceptional *imagination*.

No one can doubt it; but our agreement need not modify the conclusion we have so far arrived at. The sense of poetic greatness is precisely the same here as anywhere else: it is the consciousness of unusual richness and intensity in the life that is being communicated to us. Whether any kind or degree of poetry can exist at all without proceeding from the imagination is a question I may not stop to examine; but when *great* poetry is assumed to depend peculiarly on imagination, clearly that word

The Idea of Great Poetry

is being used in a special sense. This is the sense
implied by the old and celebrated distinction
between *imagination* and *fancy* ; and, I think, as
soon as the distinction is mentioned, you will agree
there is something in it—something pertinent, too,
to our topic. I cannot enter into the philosophy
of the distinction ; I doubt if there is more to be
made of it than a critical convenience. But, if it
is valid at all, it should be recognizable, whatever
the philosophy of it may be ; and if it has any
bearing on the idea of poetic greatness, that too
should be recognizable.

I suppose there is no passage more typical of the
work of sheer fancy than Mercutio's speech about
Queen Mab, her antics and her equipage :

she comes

    In shape no bigger than an agate-stone
    On the fore-finger of an alderman,
    Drawn with a team of little atomies
    Athwart men's noses as they lie asleep :
    Her waggon-spokes made of long spinners' legs ;
    The cover, of the wings of grasshoppers ;
    Her traces, of the smallest spiders' web. . . .
    And in this state she gallops night by night
    Through lovers' brains. . . .

Diction and Experience

Who can resist this world of gay, miniature immortality, and the intrusion of its whimsies into the serious habits of mortality ? We call this sort of thing *fancy ;* let me now put beside it an instance of what, in contrast, we should, just as certainly, call *imagination.* My instance is the famous Anglo-Saxon poem known as *The Dream of the Rood.* The poet (in what he calls " the most precious of dreams ") sees the Cross before him ; it is blazing with the encrusted light of jewels. He is shamed by the splendour. Instantly, instead of jewels, the Cross is dripping with blood ; and, mysteriously yet inevitably alternating, the Cross continues to be now a thing of dazzling glory, now a thing of loathsome horror. And then the Cross speaks. It recalls how it was once a happy tree on the edge of a wood ; but men cut it down to make an instrument of torture. They set it on a hill, and the victim is brought. The Cross longs to hurl itself on His persecutors and crush them to the ground ; but that is forbidden ; and the shuddering Cross is compelled to give the agony of death to its beloved creator.

51

The Idea of Great Poetry

Fancy is not the word for that! But wherein lies the difference between the fancy of Queen Mab and the imagination of the living and anguishing Rood? Essentially, in nothing but the range and depth and complexity of the emotion that is presented to us by the imagery. *The Dream of the Rood* puts us in possession of an incomparably richer harmony of experience than Mercutio's account of Queen Mab; and so far as the sense of poetic greatness depends on it, the distinction between fancy and imagination is simply another confirmation of the notion we have already attained to. Simultaneous riches of impression, a scope ranging from dread and pain to beauty and delight, and the harmony of all this—that is what we mean by greatness of poetic experience.

NOTE ON FANCY AND IMAGINATION

It is not easy to make out exactly what is or has been meant by the qualitative distinction between fancy and imagination. Coleridge professed his intention of settling the distinction once and for all; and after the most elaborate philosophical preliminaries, decided, when he could no

Diction and Experience

longer postpone the crucial question, to take the advice of a convenient friend and leave the matter as vague as he had found it (*Biographia Literaria*, Chap. XIII). There can be little doubt that Coleridge's mind was set working on this matter by Wordsworth's early conversation ; but Wordsworth had a special use for the word imagination ; as he expressly says, he was driven to use it, for certain sublime exercises of intuition, " by sad incompetence of human speech " (*Prelude*, Bk. VI, 592–616). This seems to be the origin of Coleridge's " esemplastic " imagination. But he extended the meaning of that portentous phrase far beyond Wordsworth's meaning ; and the difficulty is to see just what this extended meaning is—a meaning which, for all its immense extension, must never even border on that of fancy : for fancy and imagination are ' two distinct and widely different faculties." So that when Milton is said to be imaginative and Cowley fanciful, the proposition is not in the least concerned with any sort of *degree* (in which case most people would accept it), but with the use of two originally distinct *faculties*. Yet whenever Coleridge's " imagination " is at all intelligible, it is either so narrow that, as a general doctrine for poetry, Wordsworth himself felt bound to protest against it, or so wide that Cowley comes in as easily as Milton. It should be noted that Wordsworth's mature opinion, in the admirable Preface of 1815, after first classing them together as *one* of " the powers requisite for the production of poetry,"

The Idea of Great Poetry

discriminates imagination and fancy chiefly by their effects ; and it comes to very little more than Leigh Hunt's sensible definition of fancy as " a lighter play of imagination . . . analogy coming short of seriousness."

This was too simple for Coleridge. The two faculties, he allows, can co-exist in a poet ; but they are distinct for all that. If there is any meaning to be attached to his " fancy," Shakespeare was fanciful when he wrote Mercutio's Queen Mab speech. Now the one positive thing that emerges from Coleridge's discussion of the difference between fancy and imagination, or from the discussion of any other maintainer of the distinction, is this : that fancy, at bottom, is something *irresponsible*. It is just because of its invariable reliance on this notion that the distinction seems to me to have no validity whatever, except as a matter of degree. For there is no such thing as irresponsible fancy, toying with imagery for the mere sake of the images, like the tumbling about of coloured glass in a kaleidoscope. And if it is not that, if there is some significance in fancy's image-building, wherein does it differ from imagination, except in degree of significance ? But there is always at least an emotional significance, and usually much more than that, in any game the mind may play with images. A really irresponsible game would be utterly unlike the way the human mind works. However lightly you may seem to play with images as if they were counters, there is always

54

Diction and Experience

a mood standing by you, ready to put a value on the counters. Fancy is all one with imagination in function: in the shows of sense to symbolize mood—i.e. mood *at least.*

Take Mercutio's speech. " I talk of dreams," he says; and for the moment it seems easy to agree with him that these are " begot of nothing but vain fantasy." But just look what dreams they are. Every one is characteristic of the dreamer; by no means vain or irresponsible fantasy, but fantasy responsible in every case for a certain precise significance, the fantasy that is nothing but the shaping of habitual mood or ruling desire. And as with the dreams, so with their instigator—Queen Mab herself, that vision of a busy potent littleness, with her exquisite absurdity of an equipage, riding forth uncontrolled by any apparent law. Is she a mere irresponsible whimsy of the mind ? How do the fairies continue to live at all, except by *meaning* something to us ? Why, they are the symbol of one of the deepest, most universal longings that man is capable of nourishing. Anxious, accountable creatures as we are, compelled to exist in just one scale and no other, obedient to Ricardo's law of rent and the association of ideas—how could we endure ourselves if we could not now and then fantastically escape into the life of fairies and happily despise our troublesome necessities—" Lord, what fools these mortals be ? "—a remark which completely dissolves any qualitative distinction between fancy and imagination :

the fantasy of Puck here proclaims itself utterly indistinguishable from imaginative significance.

Or take another instance : Poe's *City in the Sea*. Is this not a piece of sheer fancy—a glittering pile of imagery enclosing a mere arbitrary conceit, and built up simply for the pleasure of building in such ornamental stuff ? Or perhaps it is on the borderline, or—should we rather say ? —*both* faculties are involved in the poem : it began as an act of imagination, which was handed over to fancy to be workt out. The meaning of the poem as a whole is clear enough, at any rate : death is triumphant in it. The sense of his triumph may have hardened into a conceit, an ingenuity, by being localized in a city contrived to exhibit it ; but surely in the first instance it was *imagined*—nay, " esemplastically " imagined. Surely, too, the whole conduct of the poem is very far from being a go-as-you-please of imagery : it is *designed* from start to finish. Yet is not the design covered by an encrustation of merely ornate fancy, an arabesque of far-fetcht whimsy planted on as a taking decoration ? What, for instance, have " the viol, the violet, and the vine " to do with Death Triumphant ?

I think, in such a case, the poet's mind works something in this way. It is like a man narrating his dream at breakfast. The dream would anyhow make a story sufficiently odd and striking ; but as he tells it he cannot resist improving it, to make it even more astonishing and absurd, more complete in its matter-of-fact improbability and non-

Diction and Experience

sensical coherence. We say that he *invents* these improvements—he is simply amusing himself in them. But really he is no more doing that than his brain was amusing itself with the actual dream. The dream, we know, was a symbol : some obscure shapeless impulse from the depths of his nature was embodying itself in a train of imaginary sensation. And when this symbolic substance is consciously toucht up, deliberately improved to make it more entertaining, it is thereby actually improved *as a symbolism :* whatever the man thinks he is doing, he is really elaborating still further the transformation into imagery of his original impulse. He is, by continuing in the story of the dream, continuing in the influence of its origin and carrying on the tendency of its influence. And so it is with Poe's vision of Death Triumphant. However curiously and deliberately invented the detail may seem, as though the poet meant nothing but a wanton fantasia of ornamental figures, however he may seem to be carving " the viol, the violet and the vine " for the mere delight of doing so—actually he is, with every unexpected stroke, sharpening and securing the impression of the whole vision on our minds. And the more convincing the *substance* of the vision becomes by these apparently irresponsible touches—the light from the hideously serene sea, the diamond eyes of the idols, the gaily-jewelled dead, and the rest—the more securely the whole *mood* of the vision establishes itself. The initial inspiration never leaves go of the ingeniously elaborating

57

imagery, but continues subtly to command it, however wayward and wilful it may seem to have become.

It is entirely allowable, and may be very useful, to call such poems as *The City in the Sea* fanciful. But if to call them so implies any derogation—if it implies any qualitative separation from *imaginative* work—then the word *fanciful* has, somehow or other, gone wrong : it has taken too much meaning on itself. It has, in fact, assumed the right to label a distinct faculty. Now, the faculty of fancy does not exist : it is one of Coleridge's chimeras, of which he kept a whole stable. Fancy is nothing but a degree of imagination : and the degree of it concerns, not the quality of the imagery, but the quality and force of the emotion symbolized by the imagery. Poe's poem is a masterpiece ; but the triumph of death in it has neither the force nor the quality of, say, Petrarch's *Trionfo*, not to mention *Othello*. Just as fanciful as *The City in the Sea*, and deserving the epithet for precisely similar reasons, are, for example, many passages in *The Divine Comedy* : such as the quarreling demons in the *Inferno*, or the Earthly Paradise at end of the *Purgatorio*. There is no radical change from the process of imagination in such passages ; but there is a certain limitation and agreeable specialization of emotion in them. And that is what we refer to—but it is only that we refer to—when we call such poetry the work of fancy.

58

LECTURE II

GREATNESS OF FORM. REFUGE AND INTERPRETATION

§ 1

SO far I have been mainly engaged in examining, for the signs of greatness, poetry in its momentary existence. For that is how we take it in— moment by moment : in poetry, as in everything else, we live first of all in the immediate *now ;* and in order to build up our idea of great poetry, we must begin with its momentary condition. If we have succeeded in accounting for our sense of greatness in some signal moments of poetry, still we have done no more than make a beginning. So long as we are concerned with poetry as we take it in, moment by moment, we cannot expect to get anything more than the accent or manner of greatness : the suggestion of what we may look to have when the accumulating sequence of moments is complete. If we are to lay our hands anywhere

59

The Idea of Great Poetry

on *greatness itself*, it will not be in the effect of poetry *while we are reading it ;* but in the effect it may have on us *when we have read it :* when the orderly series of poetic experiences has been collected into one final and inclusive imagination which is the compact summation of the whole : that is to say, when not merely *poetry* has come into existence in our minds, but a *poem.*

The greatness we are looking for is, therefore, strictly a property of poems rather than of poetry. The distinction might be put in a more emphatic and perhaps more familiar way, which we may find useful. For this is nothing but the distinction, so common in discussions of this kind, between Substance and Form. It is sometimes misconceived. If we regard form as something *added* to substance, a mould arbitrarily imposed on the stuff of poetry from without, it would be unintelligible to say that greatness is a property of form. But if we take form to be simply the fore-ordained and finally resulting whole impression which sums up and includes an orderly sequence of contributory impressions, then clearly it is here, if anywhere, that

Greatness of Form

the quality of greatness will reside. What we have while we are still reading a poem is its substance; but a substance which only exists for the sake of its eventual form. For the moments of a poem are only there in the interest of its design and whole intention; we read a poem for what we are to feel when we have read it. But if a poem has any effect as a whole at all, that must be because the recollection of the series of its moments impresses us as something complete in itself and self-contained, in boundaries effected by its own coherence; the recollection, that is to say, is of something which has *form*.

But, though we may agree that greatness in poetry strictly belongs to form, we must make out more exactly what this means. In any noticeable moment of poetry, we see that there is a certain set of words responsible for it. But when, at the end of a poem, we receive its final impression as a whole, there is no set of words that is directly responsible for that. It certainly comes to us as the result of all the words in the poem; but not directly. It is the organized accumulation of the whole series of momentary impressions : the impression made by all the other impressions united together. Often enough the series of impressions is so short, and accumulates into a self-sufficient whole so rapidly and simply, that the process is not noticed at all. The whole poem seems to form a single moment, and may legitimately be so described ; and we seem to take its completed impression directly from the words. Here is a poem of Allingham's which is perhaps as simple an instance of the art of poetry as we could have :

> Four ducks on a pond,
> A grass bank beyond,
> A blue sky of Spring,
> White clouds on the wing :
> What a little thing
> To remember for years—
> To remember with tears.

We are scarcely conscious of organizing these impressions into a whole. But how does, for example, *Othello* come to exist in our minds as a whole ? Not so much by a unification as by a whole series of unifications. We take first from its

Greatness of Form

enchanted language a procession of imagined ex-
periences, and these we condense into an impression
of character, and of the interaction of character ;
and this interaction we then condense into an
impression of plot ; and the plot compacts itself
into the sense of a single complex event moving
inexorably onward : and our sense of this move-
ment we condense still further, when the play is
at an end, into a final summation of impression—
some sense of life corresponding (so far as we are
capable of corresponding) with that piercing sense
of the pitiable irony of things which, stirred by an
old story he was reading, gave Shakespeare the
motive of his tragedy. It is nowhere directly given ;
it could not be expressed at all, except as the organic
inclusive impression of everything that has happened
in the play. For the play was designed for no other
end than to express this : and this final impression
is the *form* which the accumulating substance has
been forced to assume in our minds by the art
of the poet. In order to tell us what his original
intuition was, the poet has to expand it and
disintegrate it, and put it forth piece by piece in

the moments of his language ; but he also had to be providing, all the while, for its eventual re-integration into just the right harmony of total unified impression. If he could have conveyed his original intuition instantaneously from his mind into ours, there would have been no need for form, for unity would never have been lost. When St. Lewis visited Frate Egidio, they found it more satisfactory to converse directly, in a silent ecstasy of communication, mind to mind, than to discourse aloud ; for that would have been, we are told, " per lo difetto della lingua umana . . . piuttosto a sconsolazione che a consolazione."[1]   But the art of poetry consists precisely in using " lo difetto della lingua umana," in order to get, in the final result, as near as possible to the effect of such immediate communication as passed without words between the king and the friar. If " lo difetto " did not exist, the art of poetry would not exist. Since language is the medium, the first thing that must happen is breakage of unity : and the final thing should be its restoration—as poetic form.

[1] *Fioretti*, XXXIV.

Greatness of Form

And this is where we must look for the greatness of a poem.

There is a heresy, very prevalent nowadays, which goes clean against all this. It is the doctrine that poetry can only be lyrical; even epics and dramas, this doctrine supposes, can only justify themselves as poetry by their lyrical moments, their suddenly kindled raptures of imagination that detach themselves and escape from a non-lyrical purpose: a doctrine sometimes taken to its logical conclusion, that what we have been calling the form of such poems is properly to be regarded as a mere scheme for introducing lyrical moments, otherwise of no value as poetry. The opinion is not new; it was responsible for those odd compilations, once so popular in drawing-rooms, *Beauties of Shakespeare*, *Beauties of Spenser*, and the like. But it has lately taken on the airs of a dogma; and evidently it is related to the belief in " pure poetry," which I mentioned in my last lecture. We can, once more, leave out of our discussion any temperamental preference for lyrics over epics and dramas; though we should expect that preference to follow, since

The Idea of Great Poetry

the dogma can only allow form, in our sense of the word, when it is lyrical form.

It will be worth our while to look into this opinion ; for it should enable us to see rather more clearly what it is we get, or are likely to get, from the *whole* effect of a poem as distinguisht from the incidental effect of its signal moments. I will take a very familiar instance of lyrical ecstasy soaring out of and, it may seem, away from a non-lyrical— in this case, a dramatic—purpose. Faustus, in despair of satisfying his heart with earthly pleasure, after the whole range of it has been offered to him by his infernal servants, summons the phantom of Helen. Everyone knows how he greets the vision :

> Was this the face that launcht a thousand ships
> And burnt the topless towers of Ilium ?

And so on : a flight of twenty lines into the supreme regions of poetry. Most noticeably, a lyrical moment ! How it leaps out of its context, and makes a place of its own in our minds, sufficiently existing in its own perfection ! If you learn those lines by heart, you can repeat them over and over again with endless pleasure, valuing them simply for themselves, as if they were a separate poem. Or apparently so : but is the passage really detachable from its context ? Can you, for example, ever really forget that it is Faustus speaking to Helen ? If so, surely you cripple the meaning ; but if you remember that, surely also you go on to remember that it is Faustus adoring the beauty of a phantom with his feet on the brink of hell : the man who has sold himself to enjoy every bodily delight, every intellectual rapture mortality is capable of, finds that, for all the satisfaction his bargain has brought him, he might as well have stayed with " *on cai me on* " among his books ; he it is who tries to lose his despair and " glut the longing of his heart's desire " by abandoning himself to beautiful illusion ; and it is too late—-Helen herself cannot distract him from the approaching doom.

No, you may say ; this is to read too much into the passage. In the lines as they stand, secure in their own perfect achievement, Faustus has become Everyman ; this lyrical moment simply exists as an instantaneous perfection of man's worship of woman's beauty. I would answer, that certainly, at this moment, Faustus has become Everyman ; but without ceasing to be Faustus. For how is it that I can read all this into the passage as it stands in its own achievement ? Why, because I also know how it stands in the achievement of the poem as a whole. The lines are magical in themselves ; but they are much more magical in their place—in the particular context designed for them, for which they were designed. When the whole poem has completed itself in our minds, we have had their lyrical moment in all the splendor of its imagery and the intensity of its mood—in everything it can give us in itself, if it could be detacht ; but super-added even to that, the moment has given us further beauty and significance by the way it has harmonized with the rest of the story. You cannot account for everything the lyrical moment accomplishes by regarding it simply as an individual moment, existing for its own sake ; the exact rightness of its contribution to the whole event of the poem, itself adds a meaning to the moment ; beauty and significance are reflected back into it by the passions

Greatness of Form

and affairs to which it is linkt. To regard such a poem as *The Tragical History of Dr. Faustus* as justified merely by detachable lyrical moments, however splendid these may be, is to take the means for the end, to put substance above form ; and that is to ignore a vital part of what the lyrical moments themselves have to say to us : for you cannot see all they mean until you can see their place and function in the whole poem. They exist for the sake of the poem's final impression ; and by existing for that end they are impregnated by something more than their own individual and immediate beauty : they catch a glamour from the final organic beauty of the whole poem.

§ 2

This indicates more exactly the state of things we mean when we speak of a poem having form. We mean that, in the final impression made by the whole, every moment of the poem has become something more than its immediate self : every moment has affected us not only as itself, but as it contributes to the presiding characteristic unity of

The Idea of Great Poetry

the whole. In this sense, every complete poem is some sort of a microcosm—its own peculiar sort : it is a perfect system of its own interrelationships : nothing is there that does not belong to everything else there—each for all and all for each : every element in the poem is a note or tone unmistakeably helping to establish and characterize the full harmony of the poem as a single complexity of things. Ordinarily, if we follow up relationships in the world of everyday actuality, we find ourselves led endlessly on and on, out into interminable deserts. We find no finality, no terminal satisfaction, in our desire for *significance* ; for the significance of a thing is nothing but the degree and manner of its relationship with other things. But in a poem, our sense of the significance of things comes full circle, and, while we remain in the poem, is complete. We possess a self-sufficient and self-contained satisfaction, and we are delighted with the consciousness of a world which is in boundaried and rounded perfection of accord with itself.

And thus, though every poem must be its own peculiar microcosm, it must also, by virtue of what

Greatness of Form

we call its form, be some aspect, large or small, of a world eternal and universal : the ideal[1] world. For nothing can come under the rule of poetic form in an incoherent, and therefore an insignificant, manner : where everything is interrelated, everything must mean something in terms of the whole. Chance, which is essentially incoherence and insignificance, can have no place there : we experience nothing that is not measured and orderly and lawful ; and that is the experience which answers to our profoundest desires. When *poetry* achieves the perfection of its nature by becoming a *poem*, it cannot but be some revelation of the ideal world.

This is the world, then, in which the greatness of poetry will be found ; and it is a world which is ideal in its condition rather than in its matter. We have seen what sort or condition of matter it is which gives us, in the *moments* of poetic experience, the accent or tone of greatness : it is matter so

---

[1] The word, of course, is not used in its strict philosophical sense : the ideal world here is universal because it is the world of a universal desire. But this does not exclude the philosophically ideal and universal ; for it also is the world of the idea of law.

concentrated and organized as to effect an unusual richness and intensity of impression. Greatness itself must therefore be some establishment of the ideal world by means of such matter as this. When we have some notable range and variety of richly compacted experience brought wholly into the final harmony of complex impression given us by a completed poem, with its perfect system of significances uniting into one significance, then we may expect to feel ourselves in the presence of great poetry ; and the greater the range, the richer the harmony of its total significance, and the more evident our sense of its greatness. A similar effect may be given by a *series* of poems, when some connexion of theme, in idea or mood, some relatedness in the kind of harmony effected over things, enables our minds to fuse the several impressions into one inclusive impression ; but the effect can hardly be so decisive as when our minds are, without interruption, dominated by the single form of *one* poem.

We can see now what the length of a poem has to do with its greatness. Length in itself is nothing ;

Greatness of Form

but the plain fact is that a long poem, if it really is a poem (as for example *The Iliad* or *The Divine Comedy*, *Paradise Lost* or *Hamlet*, are poems), enables a remarkable range, not merely of experiences, but of *kinds* of experience, to be collected into single finality of harmonious impression : a vast plenty of things has been accepted as a single version of the ideal world, as a unity of significance. As far as unity is concerned, no less than as far as splendor of imagination is concerned, a sonnet by Wordsworth may be just as unmistakeably an aspect of the ideal world ; and it is a marvel, the range of matter in, for example, the sonnet to Toussaint l'Ouverture. But as for greatness, think for an instant of *The Iliad* as a whole, or *The Divine Comedy*. The thing simply is, that Homer and Dante can achieve an inclusive moment of final unity out of a whole series of moments as remarkable as that single one of Wordsworth's : obviously, then, irrespective of poetic quality as such, that final intricate harmony of theirs will be far richer, and so greater, than his—though by means of a unity far less direct than his, and a form less immediately impressive and therefore, no doubt, less lovely.[1]

§ 3

Just as the accent of greatness, then, is recognizable in those moments of poetic diction which give us the impression of unusually rich experience, so greatness itself will be a harmony effected by poetic form out of an unusually rich accumulation of such moments. It will be, that is to say, an unusual range and variety of experiences transmuted into a version of the ideal world—the world of things known and felt in perfect and satisfying significance. Such a version will, however, only differ from other versions in degree ; all we can say at present is, that the greatest poetry will be that which represents something like the whole gamut of possible experience, and that this will

[1] I might therefore have quite justifiably used a sonnet (one of Wordsworth's, for example, or Meredith's *Lucifer in Starlight*) as an instance in my first lecture of *momentary* greatness ; just as the argument would have indemnified me for so using the *Ode to Anactoria* if it had existed as a whole, or Dante's *Così nel mio parlar* if I had used it as a whole.

Greatness of Form

become in our minds a single infinitely rich chord of harmony.

But there are two main moods, very different in kind, which may urge us thus to idealise our experience of life—to exalt the things of this world into the condition of a more desirable world, where nothing is out of relation with the rest and all is of assured significance to us. And poetry, in its larger scope, has chiefly accommodated itself to the requirements of these two moods ; and has given us, in the result, what we may call the poetry of *refuge* on the one side, and of *interpretation* on the other. We have to decide now which of these two kinds is the more likely to effect greatness.

In either of them, we put our consciousness of life and of the world beyond the power of that senseless disaster, Chance : for there can be no feeling of chance in the experience which gives us what we long for above everything—manifest significance. But in this present world of everyday actuality, chance—the mere incoherence of things— plays, as far as we can make out, an unpleasantly important part. We may, therefore, wish to enter into poetry's perfected version of the world simply in order to *escape* from the harsh caprices of actuality. If so, we are not likely to welcome there any sharp reminder of those humiliations of our hopes and desires which make the events of life so strangely at odds with our sense of what ought to be ; though, like captured enemies, they may certainly make a very satisfactory appearance, if they can be somehow robbed of their power. On the contrary, our sense of their power ought to be enhanced and intensified if, instead of requiring a world the perfection of which is to enable us to *forget* them, we require a world the perfection of which consists in enabling us to *understand* them— to force them to yield a *meaning* for us. Thus, the poetry which gives us an experience of things beyond the reach of misfortune, may either do so by offering us a *refuge* from it, or by offering us an *interpretation* of it.

Examples will best explain my meaning ; though the aim of providing a refuge from the sense of the evils of life may seem to need little explanation. It has often been deliberately adopted ; and never

Greatness of Form

more deliberately than by Boccaccio when he wrote his *Decameron*, which, for the purpose of such a discussion as this, can only be regarded as a poem—indeed, as one of the first poems of the world. It certainly starts off with a masterly and appalling description of pestilence : but that is only by way of an emphatic symbol of the meaningless griefs and injuries which rule the world we are leaving behind. And we go with the band of young men and maidens, escaping from the infected, disordered city, into ten days of delight in quiet gardens—feasting, singing, lute-playing, dancing, strolling and, above all, story-telling : and the world of bitter reality is effectually shut out and forgotten. Does that mean that we forget there are such things as sorrow and horror ? By no means : many of Boccaccio's finest stories deal expressly with them. But he has the art to make them harmless. He induces in us a state of mind like that which Coleridge keenly notes in himself when, after a catalogue of the beauties of an evening landskip, he adds :

> I see them all so excellently fair ;
> I see, not feel, how beautiful they are.

The Idea of Great Poetry

So, in Boccaccio's tragical stories, we *see* how terrible they are, but we do not *feel* it—or not very seriously. The sheer art of narrative is with him so stringent—he keeps so intent on the exquisite linkage of events, he draws the pattern of incidents with such delicious and alert precision—that even his ostensibly sorrowful tales are, like the comic and fantastic ones—*entertaining*.

But go from this *Decameron* world to the world of his younger contemporary, Chaucer, and you enter a region in which the art of poetry has taken on a different function. If Chaucer has a tragic story to tell, he uses no art to disinfect it of distress, to make you see sorrow without feeling it ; his art is rather to make you feel what you see with unexpected poignancy—indeed, to make you feel more than you can possibly see. He may, in the end, reconcile you to the wound ; but you are to feel the stab of it first.

But poetry is hardly an escape from the insistence of our everyday world when, instead of being concerned to make painful things pleasant, it seems rather concerned, if painful things must be

Greatness of Form

dealt with, to sharpen the edge of them anew. But do they therefore remain merely painful? They do not: that is the important fact. Their emotional effect is not, as in the poetry of refuge, skilfully deflected towards an agreeable sense of things. On the contrary, it is kept ruthlessly and piercingly direct. And yet they occur in a world which, as a whole, including them and all the distress they carry, is somehow profoundly satisfactory: more satisfactory, perhaps, than any world can possibly be from which sorrowful things are excluded, or in which they are rendered harmless and entertaining. And it is satisfactory because these misfortunes have, within the nature of poetry, been given a meaning. This, then, is the poetry which accepts the evils of life because it can interpret them.

But many of the most famous triumphs of poetry have been in building cities of refuge. That has not always been the poet's intention. *The Faery Queene* may seem the very type of seclusion from the world. In no other poem can one so completely lose oneself in enchanted safety from the actual. Spenser certainly did not intend that; but his genius would not obey his intention. What he gave us is not, of course, really a poem at all, but rather an immense mound of poetry; for it is incomplete, and the form he intended for the whole can only be guessed at. Each book, however, is practically self-contained; and the sort of world he can transport us into is unmistakeable everywhere. It is a serious world; when we take refuge in it, we are by no means giving ourselves over to careless fantasy. Few poets, indeed, have been able to modulate their verses into such a plangency of wistful pathos. And yet somehow it is all harmless; beauty and virtue in distress do not, in Spenser's images of them, really wound our emotions. For they are only images, not persons; they are the figures of an allegory. It is often supposed, that the allegory is so vast and complicated, and the imagery of its embodiment so delicately charming, that enjoyment would hardly survive the trouble of understanding it: we must look on the events simply as a magical phantasmagoria. That is not quite true. Certainly, when we hear of valor

Greatness of Form

sending the groaning ghosts of his enemies to direful death, our interest is merely chilled when we understand that these are only the ghosts of moral abstractions allegorized. And when we are able to see

> One in bright armes embatteiled full strong,
> That, as the sunny beames do glance and glide
> Upon the trembling wave, so shined bright
> And round about him threw forth sparkling fire,
> That seemd him to enflame on every side ;

when we can watch the dazzling approach of this nobly-mounted knight, who

> prickt so fiers, that underneath his feete
> The smouldring dust did round about him smoke ;

how have we improved our pleasure, by learning that this handsome figure is the emblem of a classified vice ? Nevertheless, no one can read Spenser with any liveliness of attention and ignore his allegory altogether. That is where the universal sense of his incidents is placed. It is always a moral sense ; but the scale of moral values which he keeps so continually in use brings no sense of inexorable and necessary judgement, majestically presiding over human affairs. It is a serious world, but there is a spell on it : a spell that effectually seals up any deep disturbance of our emotions, and leaves us free to enjoy, simply and equably. Yes, in *The Faery Queene* we can even enjoy moral values !

But the poetry of refuge has no need to keep clear of serious, or even of tragical matters, so long as the poet has the art to make them harmless. The loveliest world poetry has ever attained to is the idyllic world of Theocritus ; a world which, after so many futile attempts to imitate it, we may judge to be inimitable. It was Theocritus who discovered the golden age. Before him, men had only heard about it ; Theocritus discovered it in the only possible way : he created it. And the extraordinary thing is that he made it a *real* world. It is a world of reality enchanted. They are real people, these shepherds and goatherds who, the instant they meet at the spring, or under the pine tree, must challenge each other to a singing match. The art of their singing is faultless : not, we feel,

Greatness of Form

because they are mere disguises of the poet, but because that is a talent real people have in the golden age. And their songs capture more of the joy of life, the inexplicable relish of earthly things, than any songs before or since. But seas and mountains and copses and flowering meadows and streams are not the only things that are familiarly radiant in their minds. They have seen the one-eyed giant sitting on the cliffs and lamenting his ugliness; they have seen the sea-nymph of his hopeless love rising mischievously out of the glittering shallows to pelt his dog with apples as it runs barking at the waves. And just as everybody to-day knows of Barbara Allen and Jemmy Green, and of her " Young man, I think you're dying "; so everybody in those days knew how Aphrodite herself, with the smile on her lips and the cruelty in her eyes, came to mock at the dying Daphnis. But they are real country people, for all that: they know their trades, and there is a rough side to their tongues. What is more to our purpose just now, they have their sorrows. But what sort of sorrow? Does it bring any discord into this enchanted world ? Listen to the serenade of the distressed goatherd :

Now I know Love. A cruel god is he : a she-lion's breasts
He sucked, and in a forest his mother nurtured him,
Since with slow fire he burns me thus, smiting me to the bone.

. . . .

O Misery ! what will be my fate, poor wretch ! Will you not
    answer ?
I'll strip my cloak off and leap down to the waves from yonder
    cliff,
Whence Olpis the fisherman watches for tunny shoals :
And if I perish——well, at least that will be sweet to you.[1]

Doubtless he will not really kill himself ; but he really is sorry for himself : his hopeless love has real and bitter pangs for him. But it is all of a piece with the world he is in—a world in which there is nothing but the beauty of things and the unending astonishment of beauty. Who would not wish to live in a world in which sorrow itself has become merely another form of beauty ? There is no need for any reconciliation to it there ; for it

---

[1] R. C. Trevelyan's translation : for English felicity, and for closeness to the Greek, by far the best known to me.

is sorrow which has been, like everything else in this world, enchanted ; it has become harmless.

One more instance : escape from this too actual world of ours is not to be mistaken when it is a purely fantastic existence poetry catches us up into : some such dazzling region as that which Shelley contrived for his Witch of Atlas to play in. What power has the world of commonplace distractions over us, so long as we remain in a world where we can possess *an aviary of odours,*

> Clipt in a floating net, a love-sick fairy
> Had woven from dew-beams while the moon yet slept ;
> As bats at the wired window of a dairy
> They beat their vans——?

But note : fantastic though it be, this version of the ideal world does not altogether omit the troublesome problems of our present world. Shelley was always a reformer, and his Witch must be a reformer too :

> And she would write strange dreams upon the brain
> Of those who were less beautiful, and make
> All harsh and crooked purposes more vain
> Than in the desert is the serpent's wake

The Idea of Great Poetry

Which the sand covers—all his evil gain
The miser in such dreams would rise and shake
Into a beggar's lap ;—the lying scribe
Would his own lies betray without a bribe.

. . . . . .

The soldiers dreamt that they were blacksmiths, and
Walked out of quarters in somnambulism.
Round the red anvils you might see them stand
Like Cyclopses in Vulcan's sooty abysm
Beating their swords to ploughshares ;—in a band
The jailors sent those of the liberal schism
Free through the streets of Memphis ; much, I wis,
To the annoyance of King Amasis.

But the Witch's zeal for reform rouses in us no
great sense of the scandals of actuality. It is all
part of the dream ; the Witch must have her pranks.
Shelley, however, can give us an equally perfect
instance of the other kind of poetry—the kind
which I say interprets life. If ever there was an
ideal world, it is the world of *Prometheus Unbound :*
for it is a vision of the world purified. But the
poem does not allow us to forget the shames and
wrongs that infest this actual life ; it enforces
them on us ; in order to reach the vision of their

banishment, we have to pass through the
magnificent agonies of the First Act. Here, if
anywhere in poetry, we may experience *ideal
evil :* in a symbolism which condenses the whole
possibility of evil into an elemental and original
malignity :

> *Prometheus :*   Horrible forms,
>   What and who are ye ? . . .
>   Whilst I behold such execrable shapes,
>   Methinks I grow like what I contemplate,
>   And laugh and stare in loathsome sympathy.
> *1st Fury :* We are the ministers of pain and fear
>   And disappointment and mistrust and hate
>   And clinging crime : and as lean dogs pursue
>   Through wood and lake some struck and sobbing fawn,
>   We track all things that weep and bleed and live. . . .
> *Prometheus :* Can aught exult in its deformity ?
> *2nd Fury :* The beauty of delight makes lovers glad,
>   Gazing on one another : so are we.
>   As from the rose which the pale priestess kneels
>   To gather for her festal crown of flowers,
>   The aëreal crimson falls, flushing her cheek,
>   So from our victim's destined agony
>   The shade which is our form invests us round,
>   Else we are shapeless as our mother Night.

In very few poets has imagination towered to

such a height of speculation as the First Act of
Prometheus Unbound. But what is it that urges
Shelley's mind thus to concentrate into living form
the sense of everything he hates ? Prometheus is
the power of love : Prometheus Bound is the world
as it is—love helpless in the power of evil. The
conclusion of the poem is the resolution of this
discord into the perfect harmony of love triumphant
and the power of evil destroyed—Prometheus
Unbound. Here is the reformer, not now escaping
from his own impotence into day-dreams of the
Witch of Atlas and her pranks, but piercing himself
with a white-hot sense of all the injuries and
imbecilities life must suffer, for the very purpose of
convincing himself that a reality above all this must
surely be destined to descend at last into being,
and replace these purposeless miseries. It cannot
be (he tells us in effect) that life is to be forever so
hideously pestered ; since what chiefly suffers in
it is the very power that can cure all ills : let but
love awake, and remember its strength, and all the
infinite persecution man has suffered from the
world will fall away like the terror of a dream :

Greatness of Form

The loathsome mask has fallen, the man remains
Sceptreless, free, uncircumscribed, but man
Equal, unclassed, tribeless, and nationless,
Exempt from awe, worship, degree, the king
Over himself ; just, gentle, wise : but man
Passionless ; not yet free from guilt or pain,
Which were, for his will made or suffered them,
Nor yet exempt, though ruling them like slaves,
From chance and death and mutability,
The clogs of that which else might oversoar
The loftiest star of unascended heaven,
Pinnacled dim in the intense inane.

That, at any rate, is the main theme of the poem ;
and it will serve as an instance of what I mean by
the poetry of interpretation. Why do I call it that ?
Is it because it is the poetry of a reformer, who
offers some explanation of life's evils, and a remedy
for them ? In that case, the value of the poem
would depend on the value we attach to the explana-
tion and the remedy ; if we cannot agree with
them, then clearly Shelley, as far as we are con-
cerned, is no interpreter. But no one need accept
his belief that love will prove a sufficient cure for
human imbecility, nor even his belief that human
imbecility is curable at all. And the notion that

mortal affairs will ever be " perfected," in the sense that evil will cease to contaminate them and will leave man as he ought to be—" just, gentle, wise " : this is a very romantic notion. The beliefs which inspired Shelley have, in fact, no more (though also no less) importance than Milton's resolve to " justify the ways of God to men " in *Paradise Lost*. Milton can scarcely be held to have made out this justification ; that resolve of his has merely an historical or psychological interest. And yet the poem which it inspired is one of the greatest and noblest interpretations of life that have ever been achieved.

But in looking for such power of interpretation as poetry may be allowed to have, we must not be led outside the nature of the art : we must not let it depend on the validity of any doctrine, idea, or explanation of life. Many poets, indeed, set out to tell us, dogmatically and decisively, what life means. But what a poet may set out to do is no great matter to us ; our concern is, what he actually did. Shelley has his doctrine, and passionately expounds it. But to what result ? That need not

Greatness of Form

depend on our belief in it ; it need not even depend on the fact that his doctrine is pleasant enough to be accepted provisionally. A similar result is just as notable in the poetry of Leopardi : the result of an equally passionate exposition of a doctrine which few would call pleasant.

About the time when Shelley was making Prometheus the symbol of man's eventual perfection through love, and of the sacred spirit in man which meanwhile, tortured but unsubdued, endures the alien tyranny of evil ; Leopardi was making of Prometheus quite another sort of symbol : the symbol of man's baseless pretension to goodness or even to any importance at all, and the symbol of Leopardi's own bitter amusement at man's regard for himself. The muses, he tells us, had offered prizes in heaven for the most useful inventions ; and the prizes had gone to Bacchus for wine, to Minerva for oil, and to Vulcan for a brass saucepan. These were awards which the gods could understand. But to everyone's surprise, Prometheus complains that no notice has been taken of *his* invention—Man. He puts an extraordinary value

The Idea of Great Poetry

on this darling invention of his ; and to make it out, carries Momus as referee down to earth on a tour of inspection. But the truth about man does not quite come up to Prometheus' assertions. I give the first incident of the tour, and the last, as specimens of Leopardi's image of life. The celestial travellers land first in the new world, to inspect man as the noble savage. They find a chieftain outside his hut, surrounded by the ceremonial reverence of his tribe. Prometheus pleasantly asks him, what he is doing.

Chieftain : Eating, as you may see.
Prometheus : You have something good to eat ?
Chieftain : Passable : a trifle of flesh-meat.
Prometheus : Butcher's meat, or game ?
Chieftain : You might call it butcher's meat : a domestic animal, anyway : my son, in fact.
Prometheus : What, was your son a calf ?
Chieftain : A calf ? No, a son like any other man's son.
Prometheus: You can't mean that ? Are you eating your own flesh ?
Chieftain : My own flesh ? No, I'm eating my son's flesh. It was just for this I got him, and took care to feed him up.
Prometheus : In order to eat him ?
Chieftain : What s surprising in that ? And his mother too, as she must be past child-bearing by now, I expect I shall be eating her soon.

92

Greatness of Form

After a little more of this, Prometheus notices the amorous way the noble savages peruse his own limbs, and thinks it advisable to inspect some more cultured kind of men. Momus, of course, is highly delighted : and continues to have the same sort of pleasure during the whole tour ; for Prometheus' invention does nothing but let him down. At last they arrive at the climax of civilization, London. A crowd in front of a house rouses their curiosity. They go in, and find, in a room full of police and lawyers and servants, a man lying on a bed with his two boys beside him. They learn that the man first shot the boys and then himself. Prometheus is interrogating a footman :

Prometheus : Killed himself and his children, you say ? What terrible misfortune had befallen him ?

Footman : None that I know of.

Prometheus : He had squandered all his money, perhaps, or was universally despised for something, or disappointed in love, or had lost his place at court ?

Footman : Not at all : as wealthy as you please, and very well thought of ; love was nothing to him, and he stood high at court.

Prometheus : Then what made him do such a desperate thing as this ?

93

The Idea of Great Poetry

Footman : He was bored—tired of life, according to a letter he
left behind him.
Prometheus : And he had no friend or relation to whose care
he could have bequeathed these unhappy children, instead
of slaughtering them ?
Footman : O yes he had ; in fact, to the person who was most
nearly related to him, he did bequeath the care of his dog.

That is the gamut of life, in Leopardi's version
of it.   Natural man breeds children for food ;
civilized man shoots his children to secure them
from a life which is, possibly, good enough for
dogs.   This is the prose—the exquisitely ferocious
prose-comedy—of Leopardi's image of life.   In his
poetry, the same governing idea prevails ; and in
a grandeur and dignity of utterance hardly to be
equalled outside Dante.   In his astonishing chorus
of mummies, the quiet of death is only stirred by
vague memories of that nightmare, life ; in the
moonlight song of his Scythian Shepherd, the
ceaseless workings of the things of heaven and earth,
always returning in their circular motion to the
starting-place, is as useless and fruitless as the vapid
circulation of human affairs.   And so on.   There
is nothing of Leopardi's which is not governed by

Greatness of Form

this idea of *pessimism*, as it is usually called—of disillusioned clairvoyance, as it might be called. English critics, unable to resist the splendor of Leopardi's art, think themselves bound to reprove the idea which rules it. But we have nothing to do now with the truth or untruth of his idea ; what concerns us is the use he makes of it. How can this be said to be any way similar to the use Shelley makes of *his* doctrine ?

Why, the thing simply is, that whatever we may think of Shelley's and Leopardi's idea of life, the poets themselves each passionately believed in his own idea. Nay, they lived in it : it was the manner of their consciousness. By means of it, they collected and organized the multitudinous confusion of life in this world into an ordered harmony of experience ; and out of their vivid sense of this harmony sprang their poetry.

And this is the poetry of interpretation. To understand why it is that we need not trespass beyond the nature of the art. There are poets who cannot endure to think of the evil in life without feeling themselves able to say why it is there : such poets as Milton and Dante. The value of this for us is that it enables these poets to take up the whole generality of life into their poetry. But there are also the poets—Shakespeare and Homer are the instances now—who can do that without, as far as we can make out, needing any explanation at all. In either case the result for us is the same. When, by whatever means, some sense of the whole possibility of life—its good and its evil, its joys and its misfortunes—is presented under the condition of poetry, it becomes *thereby* an interpretation of life.

And that must be understood in a way independent of any particular explanations, moralizings or consolations : understood in a way strictly within the conditions of poetic art. The poet, by the incantation of his language, makes his world ours : his experience becomes ours ; and if this has achieved the perfection we call a poem, it has become some participation in the ideal world. For it will have achieved a perfect coherence and interrelation of its parts, however various, into organic unity ; nothing is there which is not necessary to the whole ;

Greatness of Form

nothing can happen without reference to all the rest : the sense of this inheres in the very manner of our experience. This is the kind of experience which we most desire ; for it is wholly an affair of measure and order and law. Nothing is in it which does not carry significance ; for everything *means* the whole of our consciousness : and the significance of the whole is the designed and finite harmony, the focussed shapeliness of the whole.

Now when the matter of such experience is something like the whole possibility of life, then we have the poetry of interpretation : then we have the experience which, without needing explanation, can make the evil of life as well as the good, its sorrow as well as its joy, somehow satisfactory : for evil itself must then come to us in some profound and necessary relation with everything else : its presence is altogether in accordance with the law of the whole. Or, if the poet has an explanation, that is only his means of organizing his sense of the utmost range of life into steady unity.

It must now be quite clear, that the poetry of interpretation cannot but be greater than the poetry

The Idea of Great Poetry

of refuge ; for the harmony it effects cannot but be a fuller and richer version of life. The poetry of refuge need not exclude the sorrowful side of things ; but it must make of this a mere innocent apparition. It is always therefore a version of life made under a certain selective limitation. But no poetry can be said to interpret life, unless it includes the afflictions as well as the delights, and urges them into their fullest emotional realization. The poetry of refuge harmonizes life by leaving out or modifying the discordant tones ; the poetry of interpretation brings them in and insists on them, because it can resolve them into an ultimate harmony. The world of poetic interpretation is, then, the world of great poetry ; and it is more than a jingle of words to say, that the greatness of poetry is the greatness of its significance. For this means that its greatness is the greatness of the scope of its unifying harmony.

There are degrees of this, of course. Why is not Shelley's poetry as great as Shakespeare's, Leopardi's as great as Dante's ? The answer is simply this : both Shelley and Leopardi employ, for focussing

Greatness of Form

the whole range of life into shapely coherence, a certain limited definiteness of idea ; and in consequence their representative version of life is neither as large nor as richly substantiated as that of the poet who can achieve as harmonious a result with less selection. We must therefore now go on to a more detailed examination of the way in which poetic harmony of experience may be attained.

LECTURE III

IDEAS AND PERSONS

§ 1

I SAID that Shelley and Leopardi, with their astonishingly different ideas of life, both achieved, by means of them, a similar result : and that was a certain unity of experience, which enabled their poetry to present, as a single rich harmony of complete significance or manifest interrelation, something typical of the whole range of life, its evil as well as its good. This does not mean that such a unity is always of the same kind. Its similarity lies simply in the fact that it always makes on us some impression of greatness. But there may be as many different kinds of harmony as of individual minds ; the kind will depend not only on the particular experiences it includes, but also on the kind of idea which enables it to be inclusive at all. Great poetry will always be individual in one aspect, and universal in another.

But the idea itself may vary infinitely. It may be

Ideas and Persons

a definite moral, theological or philosophical *explana-tion* of life ; or we may be unable to define it as anything more than a dominant *sense* of life, an habitual mode of experience. It may also be something less definable still, in any intellectual terms, and yet, as we shall see, even more potently efficacious as an intensification of some large variety of life into harmonized singleness of vivid, complete, final expression, or *greatness*. But before approaching that, I wish to illustrate the way a presiding sense of life may exert its power of focussing the whole scope of a poet's experience. I will begin with the poet who was capable, perhaps, of a larger interpretation of life than any other in our modern literature—Wordsworth. To *The Prelude*, to which I shall chiefly allude, he gave, as second title, *Growth of a Poet's Mind*. From our present point of view we might call it *Growth of the Conditions of Great Poetry ;* for the process it describes is the expanding mastery of a dominant idea, and its eventual power of holding everything life can offer in an organic interrelationship and coherence.

It is not my business to formulate Wordsworth's

The Idea of Great Poetry

" philosophy." There may be something in him you can call a philosophy, though only if you rather stretch the meaning of the word. But there is obviously and very grandly in him a genius for living significantly, a power of presiding over a full harmony of things, of ordering everything he knows into one consistent and characteristic manner of experience : and of giving it irresistible expression in poetry. He did not, as Goethe did, regard nature as the garment of eternal spirit ; nature was, for Wordsworth, the very life and action of eternal spirit. Once let humanity come in as part of nature, and nothing, in such a habit of experience, can remain discordant : all must at last resolve into final harmony. This is what we mean by Wordsworth's interpretation of life. I do not stop to enquire whether " pantheism " is the right name for his ruling idea ; I do not ask whether, as philosophers, we accept it or decline it. My concern is with what it did for Wordsworth, and for the world it organized round him, and can continually organize : with the interpretation it effected for him and for us, within the bounds of poetry ; that is to say, with the shapeliness of the design it induced his world to become, that satisfying and greatly ordered design which is its own significance, and a type of the ideal. I must illustrate in its gradual enlargement the kind of harmony which Wordsworth's ruling idea enables his sum of things to impress on us, when his language can enchant our minds with the finest and deepest motions of his spirit.

He must first become vividly *conscious* of the characteristic manner of life which his mind has insensibly assumed. He shows us this happening in a famous passage, in which like magic the subtlety of the art keeps its workmanship in that exquisite precision we call restraint. It happens in response to, and so overcomes, the shock of an early sense of disharmony in things : it is when his boyhood first realized the presence of death in the world, and the blank ending of such vigors and delights as his own. This is not when he saw the grappling irons bring up the drowned corpse, and

> the dead man, 'mid that beauteous scene
> Of trees and hills and water, bolt upright
> Rose, with his ghastly face ;

the mere spectacle of death to him, " a child not nine years old," was nothing appalling : his inner eye, he tells us, " had seen such sights before." No ; it was when he brooded over the grave of the boy he had known so well and played with so often : then it was he realized the depth of his own marvellous feeling for the living earth, and consciously took possession of it, by projecting it into the memory of the lost companion :

> There was a Boy : ye knew him well, ye cliffs
> And islands of Winander !—many a time
> At evening, when the earliest stars began
> To move along the edges of the hills,
> Rising or setting, would he stand alone
> Beneath the trees or by the glimmering lake.

Then follows the thrilling description of the owls hooting—" quivering peals and long halloos and screams "—in answer to the boy's mimicry : and how the " concourse wild of jocund din " would suddenly fall silent :

> Then sometimes, in that silence while he hung
> Listening, a gentle shock of mild surprise
> Has carried far into his heart the voice
> Of mountain torrents ; or the visible scene

Would enter unawares into his mind,
With all its solemn imagery, its rocks,
Its woods, and that uncertain heaven, received
Into the bosom of the steady lake.
    This boy was taken from his mates, and died
In childhood, ere he was full twelve years old.
Fair is the spot, most beautiful the vale
Where he was born ; the grassy churchyard hangs
Upon a slope above the village school,
And through that churchyard when my way has led
On summer evenings, I believe that there
A long half-hour together I have stood
Mute, looking at the grave in which he lies.

But his boyhood knew of discords in its world stranger and perhaps even more penetrating than this : discords with the accent in them of a nameless primitive terror, suggesting in the midst of his familiar delight some insufferable discrepancy. One summer evening, he was rowing on the lake : in recounting the incident, Wordsworth characteristically notes that it was " an act of stealth and troubled pleasure." The careless reader might suppose this to be the moralist speaking ; but of course it is the psychologist—the profound and subtle psychologist who had just achieved that misprized masterpiece, *Peter Bell*. Without doubt, the mood in which the affair began had a good deal to do with its sinister ending : the grown-up psychologist could see the necessary coherence where the imaginative boy felt himself mysteriously haunted ; and it is only with the boy we are concerned. He is rowing with his eyes fixed

> Upon the summit of a craggy ridge,
> The horizon's utmost boundary ; far above
> Was nothing but the stars and the grey sky . . .
> When, from behind that craggy steep till then
> The horizon's bound, a huge peak, black and huge,
> As if with voluntary power instinct,
> Upreared its head.   I struck and struck again,
> And growing still in stature the grim shape
> Towered up between me and the stars, and still,
> For so it seemed, with purpose of its own
> And measured motion like a living thing,
> Strode after me.

The impression was so strong on him that, he tells us,

> for many days my brain
> Worked with a dim and undetermined sense
> Of unknown modes of being ; o'er my thoughts
> There hung a darkness, call it solitude

> Or blank desertion.   No familiar shapes
> Remained, no pleasant images of trees,
> Of sea or sky, no colours of green fields ;
> But huge and mighty forms, that do not live
> Like living men, moved slowly through the mind
> By day, and were a trouble to my dreams.

These nameless fears could be nothing but benefit in the end ; they could only urge his strengthening mind to enlarge the habitual manner of its experience, and thus dissolve all sense of fearful incoherence in nature.   Unknown modes of being ?   It is all an unknown mode, in the sense of being inexplicably *here :* but it is all *one* mode, it all belongs unmistakably to one vast coherence of being, it is all everywhere alive and sentient with the single spirit of the whole of things :

> To every natural form, rock, fruits, or flower,
> Even the loose stones that cover the high way,
> I gave a moral life : I saw them feel,
> Or linked them to some feeling : the great mass
> Lay bedded in a quickening soul, and all
> That I beheld respired with inward meaning.

" I gave a moral life " : by what authority ?   Is it only the personal mind that confers its specious

unity on the else unreasoned multitude of things ?
So Wordsworth's mind turns in upon itself, and
engages with the mystery there.   And to save him
from failure in this crucial test—from failure to
maintain an harmonious experience just when a
completely inclusive harmony was most required—
" rose from the mind's abyss " *Imagination*,

> the Power so called
> Through sad incompetence of human speech ;

the imagination which is the mind's ambassador to
infinitude, " our destiny, our being's heart and
home " : which is our sole commerce with that
which cannot be limited even by its own existence,
but is " something evermore *about to be*."   In the
power of this imagination the mind is

> blest in thoughts
> That are their own perfection and reward,
> Strong in herself and in beatitude
> That hides her, like the mighty flood of Nile
> Poured from his fount of Abyssinian clouds
> To fertilize the whole Egyptian plain.

And so we find it : the full diapason of this
imaginative power follows, in a strain of sublime

Ideas and Persons

confidence in the harmony of earthly things which
cannot easily be paralleled. It is Imagination, the
authentic interpreter, that has brought all the brute
turbulence of things into the living shapeliness
of a single masterful manner of grandly ordered
experience. In the Alpine pass, absolute illumin-
ation suddenly possesses him ; this earth is
the very presence of eternal spirit : *that* is the
unity of nature :

The immeasurable height

Of woods decaying, never to be decayed,
The stationary blasts of waterfalls,
And in the narrow rent at every turn
Winds thwarting winds, bewildered and forlorn,
The torrents shooting from the clear blue sky,
The rocks that muttered close upon our ears,
Black drizzling crags that spake by the wayside
As if a voice were in them, the sick sight
And giddy prospect of the raving stream,
The unfettered clouds and region of the Heavens,
Tumult and peace, the darkness and the light—
Were all like workings of one mind, the features
Of the same face, blossoms upon one tree ;
Characters of the great Apocalypse,
The types and symbols of Eternity,
Of first, and last, and midst, and without end.

The Idea of Great Poetry

But there can be no pause here. When the rapture of this attainment is quieted, the mystery of the earth has indeed been relieved, and leaves the mind free to enjoy tranquillity. But it is still Nature—the life and beauty of the earth—which chiefly engages his spirit ; the life of man is rather assumed to belong to this harmony than actually wrought into it, in

> that blessed mood
> In which the burthen of the mystery,
> In which the heavy and the weary weight
> Of all this unintelligible world
> Is lightened . . .
> While with an eye made quiet by the power
> Of harmony, and the deep power of joy,
> We see into the life of things.

But there must be no hint of discord between this beautiful harmony of nature and " the still sad music of humanity " : else will the mystery roll thundering down again ten times more formidable than before. Man must be one with nature : there must be not only no discrepancy between man's life and nature's life, there must be no division between them, in the manner of the poet's experience of them. The whole effort of man, to evil no less than to good,—even " man arrayed for mutual slaughter,"—must, like nature, be the revealed presence of eternal spirit : so certainly, that it will be, for him, the mere utterance of a truism, to say " Carnage is God's daughter." It will be the end of youthful delights :

> That time is past
> And all its aching joys are now no more,
> And all its dizzy raptures. Not for this
> Faint I, nor mourn nor murmur ;

ecstatic communing with the earth gives place to the more difficult joy of understanding man, and of taking the misery of his discordant mind up into an ultimate harmony :

> And I have felt
> A presence that disturbs me with the joy
> Of elevated thoughts : a sense sublime
> Of something far more deeply interfused,
> Whose dwelling is the light of setting suns,
> And the round ocean and the living air,
> And the blue sky, *and in the mind of man ;*
> A motion and a spirit, that impels
> All thinking things, all objects of all thought,
> And rolls through all things.

The Idea of Great Poetry

"The mind of man!"—that is the region to which the mature Wordsworth must return in order to have the whole possibility of his life ruled by his presiding genius, caught up into a single stedfast manner of experience,—"my haunt, and the main region of my song." He frees himself from all wistful regrets ; those earlier raptures, when mountains became alive and rocks " spake by the wayside," are included in a larger ecstasy : his spirit has arrived at its loftiest, most dangerous, and most triumphant exultation in its own power.

> For I must tread on shadowy ground, must sink
> Deep, and aloft ascending breathe in worlds
> To which the heaven of heavens is but a veil. . . .
> All strength—all terror, single or in bands,
> That ever was put forth in personal form—
> Jehovah—with his thunder, and the choir
> Of shouting Angels, and the empyreal thrones—
> I pass them unalarmed.   Not Chaos, not
> The darkest pit of lowest Erebus,
> Nor aught of blinder vacancy, scooped out
> By help of dreams—can breed such fear and awe
> As fall upon us often when we look
> Into our Minds, into the Mind of Man—
> My haunt, and the main region of my song.

Ideas and Persons

Without this final mastery, his experience could not have completed the harmony of its world. Nay, all the ideal loveliness man ever conceived—" Paradise, and groves Elysian "—is conditional on this conquest of the mind ; there is for Wordsworth no security of satisfaction, no certain banishment of " the fierce confederate storm of sorrow," until, in words " which speak of nothing more than what we are," he has been able to proclaim

> How exquisitely the individual Mind
> (And the progressive powers perhaps no less
> Of the whole species) to the external World
> Is fitted :—and how exquisitely, too—
> Theme this but little heard of among men—
> The external World is fitted to the Mind.

He never accomplished this noble purpose : indeed, in the prosaic tone of those last lines, we may *hear* his failure. He never achieved the poem to which he devoted his long and arduous contemplation : the poem which was to declare the World and the Mind as the two faculties of one being, the two real aspects necessary to ideal perfection : the harmony of infinite spirit with

The Idea of Great Poetry

personal experience, of the things of eternity with the things of time. In that respect, if we make exception of one poem, Wordsworth must be considered to have failed. In moments, and in many moments, he is as great as anyone ; and when we remember them, we must certainly make him the third of English poets. Owing to the peculiarity of his genius, he reaches greatness chiefly by showing us, with amazingly keen intuition, the conditions and sources of his own greatness. Even so, I have had to choose from several poems, in order to make out anything like a full account of his achievement. He never accomplished the complete existence of his characteristic harmony of experience in the impression of a single work of art : as Shelley, relying on a much less potent idea, did in *Prometheus Unbound*. That is to say, he never brought to perfection the whole life of his idea of things. But he came very near it once : and perhaps this partial achievement of Wordsworth's is the greatest thing in modern poetry ; it is surely the loftiest. Is there, outside Milton and Dante, anything really comparable with the *Ode on the Intimations of Immor-*

tality? The theme is a peculiarly specialized version of his dominant idea : but the form it gives to the process of the idea's continually widening power, and to the growth of its harmony over the whole discord of personal life in an impersonal world, makes it, at any rate, the height of modern poetic art in English. Who else has found such security of harmony in such a range of experience ? Who else has mastered English to such breadth and yet such rarefaction of power, to such a nicety and to such a grandeur of proportion, as in the *Ode?* No wonder this poet could, in *Michael* and *The Brothers*, in *Resolution and Independence* and the beginning of *The Excursion*, present the undeserved sorrows, the hopeless endurances of life, in such an aspect of deep serene significance.

§ 2

The *Ode* notwithstanding—for there, as I say, he considerably narrowed his idea of life— Wordsworth never achieved what he ought to have achieved. He can show us better than anyone else what a great poet's governing sense of life should

The Idea of Great Poetry

be, and how it should effect its government ; and the result is supremely great *poetry*. What we miss in him is the supremely great *poem ;* and we have only to mention Milton and Dante again to remind ourselves of what this means. We may perhaps admire Wordsworth's idea of life more than theirs : but, once more, it is not the idea itself, but what is done with it, that matters, as far as *poetic* greatness is concerned. Far less potent ideas than Wordsworth's have, by coming to the full perfection of their power in single poems, achieved greater *art* than anything of his except the *Ode ;* for they not only focus into one intense impression the whole life of their idea, but also—and infinitely more important—the significance of everything that substantiates the idea : the significance that comes from the mere fact of existing in a single ordered coherence of experience—in the *form* of a poem.

An idea need not be universally admirable in order to have the power of collecting into the harmony of its own complete expression such a range of things as is required for the quality of greatness in a poem. A good instance of this is

Ideas and Persons

The Wisdom of Solomon. Many interesting things
could be said of it outside our present purpose. It
is the work of an Alexandrian Jew—a Jew, that is,
who lived in Hellenism : and there is continually
in it either the fusion or the hostility of two cultures.
The difficulty of translating poetry which weds the
cloudy storms of Hebrew imagination to the finest
subtleties of Greek literary craftsmanship perhaps
accounts for a certain deliberation in the splendors
of the Authorized Version here : we feel a con-
sciously achieved magnificence, or at least a care-
fully wrought distinction, very different from the
spontaneous grandeur of the English Old Testament.
The rhythm of the original, a sort of free verse,
belonging to no assignable pattern, yet always
forming itself into distinct and noticeable cadences,
also no doubt represents a fusion of two nations,
and an extraordinarily interesting one : it is every-
thing Whitman's free verse wanted to be. But
what is more important for our purpose is the fact
that the rhapsodical abundance of the Oriental
is throughout governed by Greek lucidity and
reason. The prodigal energy which seems always

in revolt against capture into exact expression, the passion for parallelisms and amplifications, the explosions into lyrical and homiletic digression and lampooning apologue, cannot dislocate the strong outline and continuous process of the whole : it is Greek in being a work of art, a thing of symmetry and ordered design : it gives, in fact, to its turbulent matter that singleness of complex existence which we call a poem.

And it is out of the co-existence of two nationalities in one mind that the motive of the poem proceeds. The Jew is steeped in Greek civilization. He accepts and relishes the method of Greek speculation, he delights in the loveliness and nobility with which Greek language has empowered his spirit. But always at the core of his Alexandrian citizenship he remains a Jew, conscious of the divine election of his race. He cannot, like his Palestinian brother, ignore the force of the Greek ideal, nor the beauty and reality of its success. And yet, as one of the chosen people, in the midst of it he is an alien ; and he cannot avoid the contrast between the Jew's sense of God's election and the gentile sense of success in this world. Why do not the people of God's choice thrive, in the world He has made, like the mere gentiles ? His answer is, that the gentile success is nothing but a mis-understanding : " unnurtured souls have erred " ; the more completely it works itself out in their lives, the more completely they devote themselves to ultimate destruction.

For what is the central fact in the world of the gentiles ? It is death. But " God made not death." It belongs to the mere appearance of things. But the heathen, by believing in death, made it real : they " made a covenant with it, because they are worthy to take part with it." If death be the prime reality of the world, the heathen values follow as reasonable and even necessary. " Let us fill ourselves with costly wine and ointments : and let no flower of the spring pass by us." It becomes, indeed, worth while to make a success of this present world ; but to do so, Might must be Right, and the just man must be the powerful man : " let our strength be the law of justice : for that which is feeble is found to be nothing worth." And this uneasy ethic must be quick to defend itself: "let us lie in wait for the righteous, because he is not for our turn, and he is clean contrary to our doings ... He is grievous unto us even to behold."

By making his values depend on death, the gentile admittedly makes the most of this mortal world, if this world be all. What can the Jew oppose to it? Some idea, evidently, in which this world is not all. The author finds this in the idea of Wisdom. Those who make Wisdom, and not death, the prime reality of the world will find themselves at last vindicated. Not that they will be preserved from death; but short life in the knowledge of Wisdom is better than long life governed by values adjusted to the false reality of death. The servants of Wisdom may be few and oppressed, but their triumph will come; and their success is not to be measured by the way it occupies the time of this world. The heathen shall at last see that and confess it; and death, by deceiving them, will then indeed be the calamity and damnation they sought to avoid. The superb visions of Jewry triumphant and the heathen in perdition bring the preliminary

Ideas and Persons

matter of the poem to an admirably effective close, and at the same time prepare us, in the manner of perfectly assured art, for the full development of mood and idea in the noble wealth of imagery and the swiftly changing emotions that follow.

Wisdom is no perfection of the intellectual man ; it is no sort of exercise of human nature at all. It is an energy pouring into the world from beyond it, vivifying it and disposing it : " more moving than any motion." When it visits the mind of man, it is not merely government there, but the bestowal of knowledge of itself, as " the breath of the power of God, the brightness of the ever-lasting light." Wisdom is sometimes the name for the spirit of divine activity, sometimes for man's sense of this ; and often the two meanings combine. When he is speaking of Wisdom as the executant of God's will, the poet can summon up a picture as direct as anything in Homer :

For while all things were in quiet silence, and that night was in the midst of her swift course, thine Almighty word leaped down from heaven out of thy royal throne, as a fierce man of war into the midst of a land of destruction, and brought thine unfeigned commandment as a sharp sword, and standing up filled all things with death; and it touched the heaven, but it stood upon the earth.

But the grandest and most characteristic passages are those whirlwinds of vision which leave us almost bewildered by the fury of their surprising imagination, and yet in clear possession of the author's impassioned sense of Wisdom always manifesting itself in human nature and human events. The Jews, as the children of Wisdom, need not condemn this world, for all their disadvantage in it, as mere deceit and illusion. God has chosen their race to be his friends; and therefore they have Wisdom, and know what his actions mean—the actions which we call the world; they know that these actions are not all there is to be known: they have an intimacy with the Person behind and within these actions—the intimacy which alone can make them intelligible and coherent. Only because they have been so chosen for the friendship of God can they possess his Wisdom; and only because they have his Wisdom in their minds can they ᴜnderstand his actions. But the heathen can never really understand his actions. At best they are like the common run of ordinary folk trying to make out the character of a statesman. They have nothing to go on but the mere spectacle of his public life ; but they make a sort of synthesis of this after their own fashion and call it his policy ; and from his policy again, and the purpose they suppose in it, they deduce the man himself, and make to their own satisfaction an image of his personal character ; and it is all ludicrously and hopelessly wrong, as those few know (and only they *can* know) who have been admitted to the statesman's friendship and know him in his private life.

There is such a thing, in fact, as natural religion ; and it is this sort of thing. It is the religion of the best of the gentiles ; but it is nothing more than a painful synthesis of God's public acts, and can never yield a true knowledge of God himself—a sense of the personality of God. Is it the gentiles' fault ? The poet is not concerned with that ; he is sometimes quite astonisht that natural religion should fail so completely, however sincere and reasonable ; but all he is concerned to know is that his people alone have been chosen by God to be his friends ; and therefore they alone have Wisdom, and the secret of God's personal purpose in the world. There is, indeed, along with natural religion, a natural wisdom ; it is no more than an honest skill in the mere matter of things, but eternal Wisdom has a certain sympathy for it. It is the best thing the gentiles possess, but as far below the Wisdom of the Jews as natural religion is below election to the friendship of God. The poet instances boat-building and seamanship ; and in a strain of ferocious amusement contrasts this natural wisdom with the capital imbecility—and that is as much as to say the capital sin—of idolatry. If a man must say his prayers to woodwork, why not choose such beneficently skilful woodwork as a seaworthy ship, rather than the skilful folly of a coloured figure ? And his satire proceeds to give, still with amused contempt, and perhaps for the first time, a rational explanation of idolatry.

So, after largely expounding what Wisdom is, and the understanding of this troublesome world which it confers on the chosen people, the poet goes on to expound what Wisdom does, and the fortune it confers on the chosen people by its management of events. The magnificent rhapsody on the history of Jewry shows all this nameless poet's astonishing power. It is, as it were, the secret history of things ; it shows us not the process of events as the gentiles see it, but as the privileged Hebrew understanding sees into it ; for only the Jewish mind inspired by Wisdom as divine instruction can see how mysteriously Wisdom, as the divine energy of things, favours the Jewish nation. A noble metaphor, at first only suggested, and at last proclaimed with unforgettable force, elaborates this. Just as death, the calamity of the heathen, is a blessing to the Jews—" in the sight of the unwise they seemed to die . . . but they are in peace," —so " the whole creature " might be changed, " serving the peculiar commandments, that thy children might be kept without hurt. . . . Where water stood before, dry land appeared . . . and out of the violent stream a green field." Things are made harmful and appalling to the enemies of the Jews even while the Jews are going unscathed through the midst of them : " for them the bitings of grasshoppers and flies killed, neither was there found any remedy for their life ; . . . but thy sons not the very teeth of venomous dragons overcame. . . . For the creature that serveth thee, who art the Maker, increaseth his strength against the unrighteous for their punishment, and abateth his strength for the benefit of such as put their trust in thee."

Wisdom holds the world like a psaltery, and on its elements and forces can play comfortable or terrible chords. The instrument is the same, and the player is the same ; but the mood of the player changes with those for whom he plays ; and from the same events he may bring fearful music for the heathen, and then, turning to the Jews, melody like heaven opening. The grand type of this, and of all Wisdom's disposal of the affairs of men, is given in the account of the plagues of Egypt : language, whether we look at the English or the Greek, has seldom conveyed such complicated sublimity of imagination as this.

My abstract of this extraordinary poem may

seem to have made it chiefly an affair of *thought ;*
but that is only because it was important to my
purpose to extricate the governing idea of the poem.
The value of the poem is certainly not in the logic
of its thought, but in the passion and imagination
of its thought : that is to say, in the vivid experience
of the world to which this thought gives its
governance and its form. I wisht to bring before
you the immense scope of this idea of life, of this
intricately organized manner of experience ; and
to give you some notion of its unifying power. In
itself, no doubt, the idea is so harshly sectarian that
it must be decidedly repellent. This is what the
fierce and baffled prejudice of a Jew sees ; yes, but
he is a Jew who sees the whole fact of life, and sees
it as a perfectly designed order of things. We
acknowledge the greatness of the poem even while
we dislike its idea ; for the idea has irresistibly
come to life in our minds ; and in so doing has
given us a sense of necessary harmony, whatever
the particular version of it may be worth, somehow
prevailing through the whole vast riches of human
experience, through evil as well as through good,

and uniting it all at last into the shapely significance of the world we so profoundly desire. To that end we are ready to accept any means.

§ 3

Something similar is to be seen in *Paradise Regained*. The ruling idea is much less obviously harsh and repellent, though it has some awkward difficulties, and at one point forces Milton to say things which should have been repugnant to him. What we admire in it, however, is its power of firmly holding an ample comprehension of life in the scope of its organization, and of thereby impressing on us its harmony of things as a type of the ideal world of perfect interrelation and significance.

The Quaker Elwood took to himself the credit of suggesting *Paradise Regained* to Milton, as the sequel of *Paradise Lost ;* but the suggestion was superfluous. It appears that Milton had for long been attracted by the notion of a short discoursing epic, for which he cites the *Book of Job* as a model— a debate between opposed principles on the ultimate values of things. The characteristic thing in

Ideas and Persons

Milton's idea is the absolute and irreconcilable nature of the opposition. Satan as the maintainer of worldly values, and Christ representing spiritual values, can stand on no common ground : one or the other must be a usurper in existing at all. Either set of values supposes in its success the destruction of the other. This is in striking contrast with the idea of *The Wisdom of Solomon*, in which the apparent opposition between worldly and spiritual life only needs to be understood in order to resolve the discord : this world being, so to speak, merely the public policy of God which brings no sense of contradiction to those who are in private intimacy with his spirit. The contrasts between the entangled complications of *Wisdom* and the lucid shapeliness of *Paradise Regained*, and between the styles of imagination in the two poems—the scarcely governable frenzy of the one, and the noble case of the other—these contrasts require no remark. Milton, it seems, when he arrived at the composition of *Paradise Regained*, had but to sit back and think, and his thought assumed instinctively the intricate symmetry of a work of art ; he had but to talk at

I 129

The Idea of Great Poetry

his ease, and the simplest language became enchant-
ment and majesty. This, of course, is the illusion
produced by craftsmanship when it has become
second nature. Certainly Milton needed all his
craftsmanship here, where the gorgeous elaborations
of *Paradise Lost* would have been improper, and
where an idea so simple and inelastic as the hard
division of values into worldly and spiritual had to
be transformed into the condition of poetry.

It has often been noticed that the Satan of
Paradise Regained—Satan as the spirit of worldly
success—is the spirit of vulgarity : spiritual success,
for Milton, could only be aristocratic. That is one
of the means which Milton uses to make his idea
come to life in our minds ; but it is also his way of
enlisting our sympathies on the right side, and of
making us rejoice with him in spirit's victorious
issue from its duel with the world. Satan himself
is a most mannerly disputant, and his values always
have an air of dignified reasonableness—until they
are contrasted with the values Christ maintains
against them ; and instantly then we recognize the
unconscious and incurable instinct which Satan

represents. Each temptation would, if it had succeeded, have been a victory for vulgarity. The very first bout of the contest makes this unmistakeable. After the dreams of Christ hungering in his sleep,

> Sometimes that with *Elijah* he partook,
> Or as a guest with *Daniel* at his pulse ;

it was a pitiable vulgarity in Satan to rely on such gorgeous ostentation of power over the whole world's edible resources, course after course of pompous cookery, with music sounding and handsome attendants inviting and all manner of luxury accompanying, in order to break down Christ's fasting strength. The passage is one of singular beauty ; precisely because Milton could not make his effect, unless the feast had been delicious to every appetite of the flesh. Therein consists Satan's misfortune in this duel ; the more he displays, and the more loftily he displays, the power of the world, the grosser its contrast with spiritual values. Does he insist that spirit is helpless in the world without wealth, since wealth is power ? But power over the world has no sense without the power which

> Governs the inner man, the nobler part ;

that is the only power that matters, and nothing can assist it ; for it is the power of the spirit. He may plead that glory and the praise of men make the proper motive of action. For how can nobility be selfish ? Yet who gains by private virtue but the possessor ? And how can even he be sure of his merit, without public approbation ? He is answered, that noble action looks for no assurance outside itself, nor needs to stir the people, the " herd confus'd," the " miscellaneous rabble " :

> To live upon thir tongues and be thir talk,
> Of whom to be disprais'd were no small praise :
> His lot who dares be singularly good.

So with the offer of either of the two empires that then divided the world : an offer made in that strain of vast panorama for which Milton has no rival. Rational purpose requires rational means : with Parthian militarism or Roman civilization entirely at his command, Christ could do everything he wisht, and impose his spiritual values irresistibly. But what can spiritual effort have

to do with the Parthians' " cumbersome luggage
of war,"

argument
Of human weakness rather than of strength ?

As little as it has to do with Roman " grandeur and
majestic show,"

though thou shouldst add to tell
Their sumptuous gluttonies and gorgeous feasts.

Whatever good there was in Rome originally has
been stifled : and why ? Simply because Rome
did achieve worldly success ; and that killed all its
chance of spiritual success. There is no possibility
of accommodation between the two sets of values :
spirit can only live in matter by declining the whole
authority of the material world.

Satan now becomes the embodiment of the
business sense. Things offered free are, in his
vulgar mind, despised : a price should always be
asked. The price he now demands is, indeed, a
nominal one, but sufficient to show that what he
offers is worth considering.—Sufficient, certainly !
For the price thus impudently named—that Christ
should go through the form of worshipping Satan—

133

The Idea of Great Poetry

is nothing but a symbol, that spirit *requires* for its success material means. If spirit were to admit that, it would cease to exist as spirit.

Rome now yields to Athens; and it is here that spirit's rejection of the world becomes unreal; something that Milton, " in the cool element of prose," could himself hardly have maintained. The spiritual life which rejects the empire of truth and beauty seems to empty itself of meaning. But the governing idea of the poem overrides these doubts: it is determined on its own complete victory.

And now, after the night of terrors, which serves as an artillery attack on morale, comes the final and the most dangerous assault. Let Christ *prove* himself the Son of God, and show the world what he means by the claim. For who is not, in one sense or another, the Son of God? Even Satan may be so called: the title " bears no single sense ";

> The Son of God I also am, or was,
> And if I was, I am ; relation stands ;
> All men are Sons of God ; yet thee I thought
> In some respect far higher so declar'd.

134

Ideas and Persons

What harm can there be, what possible degradation, in proving to the world what else must remain mere assertion ?

> Cast thyself down ; safely if Son of God.

But spirit knows its own virtue, and is content with that :

> Tempt not the Lord thy God, he said and *stood*.

Why should spiritual power prove itself at all? Its values would gain no authority by convincing anything outside itself, for only spiritual life is concerned with them and can delight in them. In any case, to convince the power of the material world would be to admit the right of the material world to be convinced, whereas, for spirit, it has no right to exist at all. With the defeat of this last and subtlest attempt to make spirit submit to matter, Christ's victory is celebrated in a passage which for once challenges comparison with the most elaborated art—simile inlaid with simile—of *Paradise Lost ;* and with a stroke of art more marvellous still, conclusion is given to the whole poem in lines of quietest simplicity : the vast affair we have lived in so greatly and so intensely resumes the pathos of mere humanity :

> hee unobserv'd
> Home to his Mothers house private return'd.

§ 4

The distinction between " world " and " spirit," with the separation of values into two codes, is perhaps one of the most vexatious things man's mischievous intellect has ever invented : and here is a poem written to celebrate this very thing—a poem, moreover, which may plausibly be said to accentuate the troublesome nature of the distinction just where it seeks to give it an absolute sanction. All this may be said, and the poetic greatness of *Paradise Regained* is not thereby impugned. We do not have to accept Homer's ethical and religious ideas in order to acknowledge the greatness of the *Iliad ;* why should we make any more difficulty over Milton's beliefs ? It is what he did with them that matters. The idea of life which governs *Paradise Regained* is one which could not be brought into imaginative existence at all without involving a vast range of human experience : and Milton's poetry realizes to the utmost the immense possibility of speculation which surrounds the idea. And all this comes to us under the strict and living governance of the idea ; so that it exists in our imaginations not only as a noble wealth of life, but also as a firm organization of life : and in the things we know, we welcome that sense of perfect mutual relevance which we desire.

But now we come to a further stage of our enquiry. Why has common consent never allowed *Paradise Regained* to be as great a poem as *Paradise Lost ?* Is it that the idea of the earlier poem is one of even larger comprehension than the idea of the later poem ? Certainly the idea of *Paradise Lost* is one of the eternal ideas : no conceivable criticism can lessen its force. How can there be individual existence except as a kind of forlorn revolt against the general existence of the whole ? And yet how can the general existence of the whole be thought at all except by an individual thinker ? How can we have the sense that we are, in our own right, *ourselves*, and yet, just as unmistakeably, also have the absolutely irreconcilable sense, that we are particles in one single unbreakable process of things ? Fixt fate—free will : that is the inmost theme of *Paradise Lost ;* with the rider, that the pride of the individual in his revolt against the general law is the essence of what we call evil, and yet is the sole source of his dignity as an individual. Original sin : that is the second eternal truth (it is merely another aspect of the first) which inspires and governs *Paradise Lost.*

That these are ideas superior in themselves to the motive of *Paradise Regained* will not be denied : and they are not only superior in themselves—a fact, for us, of quite secondary importance—but their complete substantiation requires an even grander range of thought, of feeling, of imagination, of knowledge. But a poem is not only great by reason of the richness of the experience it induces in us : equally important is the intensity of its impression. And *Paradise Lost* is as far above *Paradise Regained* in its intensity of imaginative life as in the richness of this. And who can mistake the reason ? What is it that lives in our minds when *Paradise Regained* has completed itself there ? It

Ideas and Persons

is the *idea* of the poem. But what lives in our minds when *Paradise Lost* has completed itself ? It is the figure, the *character* of Satan—with all the significance of the poem surrounding him like the atmosphere of a personal prestige. How can the life of an idea compete in impressiveness with the life of such a person as the Satan of *Paradise Lost?*— a life as vast as anything the mind of man has ever conceived, and yet more vividly known to us as a person than anyone we are likely to meet in the actual world ; for indeed it is we ourselves who give, urged and governed by Milton's art, the life we know in this Titanic figure.

Now Satan is a very distinct personality in *Paradise Regained.* I called him the spirit of vulgarity there ; and so he is. But of course he is much more than that : the spirit of a single quality can never be a *person ;* and there could be no more convincing revelation of depths of personality than Satan's answer to Christ's formidably thrusting question :

> What moves thy inquisition ?
> Know'st thou not that my rising is thy fall,
> And my promotion will be thy destruction ?

Satan, " inly rackt," replies : " Let that come when
it comes " ;—

> I would be at the worst ; worst is my Port,
> My harbour and my ultimate repose :
> The end I would attain, my final good.

A keen and awfully ironic refinement, this, on his
original manifesto—his famous exclamation of
" Evil, be thou my good ! " And we get a quite
different insight into his personal quality when he
reminds us of his later progeny, Mephistopheles, by
the fit of gibing that takes him at Christ's disdainful
rejection of glory, " the people's praise." This
aristocratic contempt of glory, he says, ill becomes
one who boasts himself the Son of God ; for
certainly, God is no aristocrat : " He seeks glory ! "—

> Glory he requires, and glory he receives
> Promiscuous from all Nations, Jew or Greek,
> Or Barbarous, nor exception hath declared :
> From us his foes pronounc't glory he exacts.

Yet the difference between this Satan and the
Satan of *Paradise Lost* is unmistakeable. In *Paradise
Regained*, he is wholly subordinate to the idea ;

the idea is the thing there, and Satan belongs only to
one half of it, and that the least important half, as
the poet conceives it. That is why Milton could
here at last draw the spirit of evil in a style satisfac-
tory to Puritan conscience : a thing which he can
hardly be thought to have done in *Paradise Lost*.
Needless to say, since we are speaking of an art so
consummate as Milton's, that is exactly the Satan
required for *Paradise Regained*.

But in *Paradise Lost*, Satan *is* the idea : the
character of Satan is the presiding thing ; he is
the essence and force and scope of the originating
motive ; and in his character, in the immense
consistency of his superbly personal energy, resides
the significance of the whole poem ; for he is the
focus of it all, and out of him and his destiny
radiates that mutual relevance of things, which is
what we call significance. The whole informing
power of the idea, with its wealth of accompanying
imagination, and its gamut of emotions, has been
concentrated and transmuted into the presence of
a living person ; and how else could such a profound
sense of the basic, the metaphysical contradictions

in human existence as Milton's, have been presented
in any harmony of impression, unless as the com-
plex harmony of a vast personal life ? Here is the
very quintessence of individual existence, with all
possible pride in its ability to stand out against
the mere universality of things, its determination,
even in the midst of defeat and destruction, to be
itself and its own law, in defiance of the Almighty
law of the world ; here, raised to its highest power,
is the dual consciousness of individual life—of
what it is and what it is against—which constitutes
both its excellence and its original sin : here, in a
word, is *Fixt fate—free Will*, the idea of *Paradise
Lost*, come to life, and to such a potency of personal
life, that it surrounds itself with a world that is one
immense tragic harmony—everything that is symbo-
lized by *the Fall of Man :*

> What though the field be lost ?
> All is not lost ; the unconquerable Will,
> And study of revenge, immortal hate,
> And courage never to submit or yield :
> And what is else not to be overcome :
> That Glory never shall his wrath or might
> Extort from me.

Ideas and Persons

§ 5

The art of poetry, in its widest sense, can do nothing more impressive than the creation of human character. It is never so alive, it never makes such seizure on our minds, as when the result of all its verbal and imaginative technique is our entrance into the life of a character, into a vividly personal form of experience. And so it is with *great* poetry. It is never so great, because never so impressive in its quality of greatness, as when its harmony of some large range of experience comes to life in us in the form of a personal figure. And besides the superior command over our imaginations and sympathies which it then has, two other advantages in this may be mentioned. The idea which has turned into a person is far less liable to the impertinence of logical criticism than the idea which, for all the wealth of its substantiation, remains an idea : the essential thing, the impression of a harmony, is far less likely to be interrupted by disagreement with its means, when the harmony comes by sympathy with the life of a character, than when it

143

must, to exist at all, somehow stir our philosophy. We are less likely to object to the impiety of Satan or the villany of Macbeth than to the opposition of values in *Paradise Regained* or the pessimism of Leopardi.

There is a second and even more important advantage. By the creation of vividly personal and credible characters, impulses may be transferred alive into our minds which otherwise could not have been given to us at all. The range of matter is therefore larger—the scope of the technique is wider—and there is in consequence the opportunity of greater poetry, when its government is the sense of unity in a subtle and complex personal life, than when it has the more rigid unity of the intellectual life of an idea. Analysis will never exhaust all there is in the impression made on us by the character of Satan ; but that which evades analysis is as lively in our minds as that which can be captured. Even Milton could not have told us in direct language all that moved him in the inspiration of *Paradise Lost*. But his language can create Satan's character in us ; and in the whole behaviour of that marvellously personal figure, nuances too fine and feelings too deep for direct statement can come unmistakeably to life in us.

We could, no doubt, if minute classification were here worth while, make out many degrees and kinds of greatness in poetry. But the world seems pretty well agreed as to what it requires in the supremely great poems. It requires the kind of significance which is given by characteristic personalities: by unique personalities which nevertheless live universally in our minds as representatives of main aspects of human nature: by Milton's Satan; by Job; by Prometheus; by Achilles and Hector; by Hamlet, Lear, and Macbeth; by Faust; even by such deliberately economized characters as Tartuffe and Harpagon; or by the still more peculiar effect, when the poet himself is the character his poetry creates. This last, however, must be postponed till we have seen more exactly what character in great poetry involves.

LECTURE IV

TRAGIC GREATNESS: THE HERO

§ 1

THE mere presence of vividly credible and richly endowed character in a poem does not necessarily make the poem great. If it did, we should have to call *Henry IV* one of the greatest of Shakespeare's plays, which is certainly not what we do call it. Who would think of comparing *Henry IV*, for greatness, with *Macbeth*, *Lear*, *Hamlet*, *Othello?* Yet is not Falstaff as great a character as the central figures in these plays? Has he not as demonic a power as they have of taking possession of our minds, and of compelling us to live in all the riches and intensity of his many-sided genius? Yes; he is great poetry; but only in the sense of being a great incident in poetry; not even he can make *Henry IV* a great *poem*. His creation was a magnificent superfluity; he is not needed for the theme of the play: or rather,

146

he is a disproportionate exuberance of one part of the theme. In a sense, no doubt, he dominates the play ; but in the sense that, while he and his fortunes are present, we *forget* the rest of the play— not in the sense that in him and his fortunes all the rest of the play is collected into a single unifying purpose.

Let me summarize for a moment. When poetry is called great, it is not only on account of the *range* of its matter, though that is important : for we could not call poetry great which did not face the whole fact of man's life in this world, its wickedness and misery as well as its nobility and joy. But its greatness also consists in the *organization* of its matter—and that, remember, is the evil as well as the good of life—into some consistent shapeliness or coherent unity of final impression ; so that, whatever means have been taken to effect it, we have at last the sense of belonging to a life in which everything is related to everything else, in which nothing can intrude by chance, but all is required, even the evil is required, in the interest of the whole : nothing can there occur which does not belong to, and assist into being, one inclusive, harmonious orderliness of existence ; and this, in the very manner of our acquaintance with it, is therefore throughout significant to us : for everywhere there is meaning in it, since everywhere there is unmistakeable connexion. To give us some distinct and keen experience of this way of existing is the true sign of greatness in poetry : and it can only be complete when the nature of poetry has been perfected into a poem.

The poet, in fact, has had some means of focussing all the energies of his imagination into a single composite ardor of ideal experience : it is because, profoundly delighting in some special sense of the instant values of things,[1] or in some habitual

---

[1] And I should add, if I wisht to be meticulous, sometimes also in the instant valuation of his values ; but it would only be for the purpose of collecting all æsthetic valuation as instant and intuitive. Keats, for example, had his immediately intuited values of things, and rebuked Shelley for not sharing them, or for not being content with them. Shelley delighted in reasoned values ; but it was a radiantly æsthetic delight in them ; it was an intuited valuation of these rational values, the instant sense of his happiness in them, that his poetry so often expressed.

148

manner of feeling and understanding, he has been moved to give to this a life as full, as radiant, as many-coloured, as he can contrive ; and thus his imagination has supplied not merely energy to urge his poem and keep it going, but also government to manage it and keep it to one purpose. His ruling sense of things may have defined itself in his mind into a quite explicit idea of life ; and in that case, when we feel everything in his poem contributing to its complete and vigorous vitality, it is not so much the idea itself that impresses us as its power of digesting and organizing the mass of things. Nor is this really at all contrary to the poet's intention ; for his peculiar sense of life, and whatever idea may have grown into definition out of it, are nothing but his mode of appreciating his own instinctive conviction of harmony in the whole of things. Thence the poet's idea of life arose, and to that his idea finally takes us in his poem.

But the poet's sense of life may also present itself to his mind, not as a definite idea, but as the vividly characterized experience of a person ; and when by his art he hands over to us both the action

which he sees and the inmost secret which he feels
in his imagined impersonation of the significance
of things, everything follows that has been asserted
of the life of ideas in poetry : but with this addition,
that now we acknowledge a life incomparably
richer, more intense, more persuasive, and at the
same time of a far wider and subtler reverberation.
This is why the world has regarded as the supremely
great poems those which collect their whole sense
of life—and everything for which an idea of life
may stand—into the behaviour and spirit of
memorable personalities.

Think, for example, of the *Iliad*. Try to
recollect its significance ; and what do you find
yourselves recollecting ? Surely Achilles and Hector
and Diomedes, Andromache and Helen. Achilles,
no doubt, is the presiding figure : in him chiefly
lives Homer's sense of the goodness of life. It is
personal ascendancy. Homer has no need to
explain what this is, nor to say why it is good.
There it is, for him : heroic virtue, the one thing
in life good past all mistake, the unaccountable and
irresistible *prowess* which men like Achilles announce

by their mere presence before us. The divine figure of Pallas Athene, towering beside him with her immortally blazing eyes, is not Homer's attempt to account for Achilles ; it is his sublime metaphor of inexplicable virtue.

There are, of course, innumerable things to be praised in the texture of the poem ; and we cannot praise them too much, so long as we remember that they *are* texture, and serve but to clothe the poem's action. There is, for example, the general sense which Homer conveys of the reality of his story to him ; and this is important, for it means that he never seems to be inventing, in order to embody the significance he feels in things : this always has the momentous air of being simply the real meaning of real things. He is recounting what, for him, actually happened, in the idiom which will best convey that (as, for instance, in the figure of Athene just mentioned) ; and his sense of the values of life emerges unproclaimed, from the mere manner of his story. This is the true epic quality : but nowhere else does such a gusto in the recording of actual affairs yield such an inevitable discovery of spiritual significance. On the other hand, there is the exquisite finish of the detail, especially in his similes : forest fires at night on the coastwise mountain, reddening the sea for miles ; flocks of birds settling on the marshes ; flies in the milking sheds ; the curve of breaking waves ; clouds in the night, opening out to reveal the unspeakable stars. No poetry, except Dante's, pours out such a lavish of exquisitely wrought treasure. And still it is only the texture of the poem ; and to admire the *Iliad* for its texture is like admiring a mountain for its colour. The colour may be astonishing ; but the really mountainous thing is the attitude of its mass. So with the *Iliad ;* whatever else we admire in it, the thing most admirable must always be the shapely mass of the poem as a whole.

Now this notable form which the poem assumes when it is complete in our minds—what is it but the way Homer's sense of the heroic in life has moulded the whole matter of his story, from its height of exultation down to the bottom of its agony and despair, and mastered all the tumult of its events into one final and inclusive harmony ? But

Tragic Greatness : The Hero

why is it that the total impression of the *Iliad*—the whole pattern of its tragically noble world—has such an extraordinary power over our minds ? It is because the agency by which it is effected comes to us in a form so absolutely commanding : for it comes to us in the form of radiantly living persons. We may make, if we like, some sort of abstract of it : we may even formulate the inspiration of the *Iliad* into a fairly definite idea. The goodness Homer sees in life, we may say, is the goodness man must make of things evil. Fate is the only disposer, and the ignominy of death is the only end. But man can make of these his own personal *danger ;* and by so doing can give himself a sense of personal value. For he can face the danger, and be its master even if it kills him. War is the type of the evil of life ; but it is also the type of the good man can make of it. In war, he has pre-eminently the joy of asserting his own value, and of seeing it reflected back to him by the honour of his fellows. But if, as happened with Achilles, the honour he has deserved is taken from him, life becomes shameful, for his prowess is despised, his ascendancy is useless. We may go on elaborating our abstract until we find ourselves describing the plot of the poem. But however accurately and faithfully we do it, we tell ourselves nothing of the force which Homer's sense of life really exerts on us. For it never comes to us as an idea at all ; it comes to us as Achilles and Patroklos, Hector and Andromache, Agamemnon and Priam. It is in its creation of these superbly personal yet profoundly symbolic figures that the security of the *Iliad* lies, as one of the supremely great poems in the world.

Contrast this quality of effect with that of *The Dynasts :* the two poems have enough in common to make their contrast justifiable. In *The Dynasts*, too, war is the type of the evil of man's life ; and it has, for Hardy, at least this good also : it forces us to face the essential things, it compels us to realize, in appalling concentration, the sort of existence we belong to—an existence, says Hardy, that takes not the least account of its individuals, but is simply concerned with going on, with keeping up its remorseless and purposeless elaboration of the destiny of the whole. And this is brought before us in the true epic manner, as the result of recounting solid reality, things that actually happened. Nor has the *Iliad* itself a greater range of matter than Hardy's chronicle of the Napoleonic Wars ; and as this is compacted into tremendous unity of final impression by a singularly potent idea of life, the result is a poem which can only be compared, and will only be compared by the criticism of the future, with the great poems of Europe. For any true comparison in English literature we must go back to Wordsworth, or even, for the wholeness of its effect, to Milton. Yet the very nature of its idea prevents *The Dynasts* from exerting such an effect as *Paradise Lost* or the *Iliad*. For no kind of personal life could ever be its symbol ; since the whole force of the idea is its denial of any personal life at all, except as the most trifling of illusions. As, from the circle of the Phantom Intelligences, we look down on the tormented earth, we see " innumerable human figures busying themselves like cheese-mites " ; we see transports and battleships floating before the wind " like preened duck feathers across a pond " ; and three whole armies become " motions peristaltic and vermicular, like three caterpillars." And when to this mere height of vision is added the penetrating clair-voyance of the Intelligences, we see the whole multitudinous world as one of the Immanent Will's " eternal artistries in circumstance " ; an artistry which here happens, " in skilled unmindfulness," to have produced in its pattern the perfectly futile decoration of life individually conscious—or, as Hardy fiercely puts it,

> the intolerable antilogy
> Of making figments feel.

But the Will of the whole, the Immanent Will, makes nothing of that ; it is a sublimely entranced automatism, heedlessly operating its incredibly intricate handicraft :

> So the Will heaves through Space and moulds the times
> With mortals for Its fingers. We shall see
> Again men's passions, virtues, visions, crimes
> Obey resistlessly
> The purposive, unmotived, dominant Thing
> Which sways in brooding dark their wayfaring :

a Will, however, which is only " purposive " in the

sense that it has the purpose of going on, and continuing its own existence, " raptly magnipotent."

The grandeur of *The Dynasts* seems to me undeniable ; and perhaps no better instance could be found of the greatness of poetry coming from the rigorous mastery of an idea over the whole unruly fact of life. But it is a mastery which, whatever its authority, can never possess men's minds like the presence of a Satan or an Achilles. The idea of life which will not allow individuals to be more than the " fingers " of universal Will has of necessity entered a self-denying ordinance against the achievement of supreme greatness in poetry : the greatness of the living symbolism of vividly personal figures.

§ 2

The poet, however, who goes to legend for his material is likely to find himself provided from the very beginning of his work with the first condition or rudiments of that achievement ; for if it is a myth which he takes in hand, he certainly starts with a symbolic figure. Probably it is a figure of no very distinct personality ; and probably too its significance is not very distinct either. The poet's art must be not only to widen and deepen and enrich the significance and make its force un-mistakeable (and he may even alter its direction); it must also effect that utmost intensification of this which comes of making it live as an absolute personality. Much criticism has been spent on Goethe's *Faust*, with varying result ; and it seems clear that, while it is acknowledged to be, beyond question, one of the great European poems, it has not won common consent to a place among the few supremely great poems. It needs no remarkable analysis to show us the reason.

Like Hamlet and Don Juan, the figure of Dr. Faustus first makes his appearance as one of the myths of the Dark Ages. Faustus is something of a Prometheus for the Dark Ages : he is the vicarious sacrifice—not, like Prometheus, for life itself,—but for intellectual life ; for he is the embodiment, the living symbol, of the idea, or rather perhaps the feeling, as old as man himself, that progress in knowledge is evil, or at least to be punisht. Well—in spite of the fact that Universities exist respected and perhaps revered—is not the intellectual appetite one of the evils of life ? How comfortable and sedate life might be, if only intellect would keep quiet ! And what do we gain from its meddling ? Always some new disappointment—what Dante called " the eternal grief " of the philosophers ! No wonder the Dark Ages (as we call them), discovering afresh both intellectual ambition and its doom—that it must always frustrate itself just at the moment of its success—in their sensitive simplicity took this as a positive torment. For intellectual progress consists merely of successive failures to be that which it exists by desiring to be — *certainty* : and the farther it goes the better it knows this. We cannot even nowadays be certain of our own uncertainty. All we know is, we can never get outside our own version of things and see whether it be right or wrong : and insatiably we long to do so, and to see things as they are. Besides, this intellectual ambition of ours, and our desire of knowledge for its own sake—what is it but a kind of revolt against the original earth of our

159

being ? And what else is evil but revolt ? There is no evil in nature ; for nature is obedience : only man has the power to rebel.

Yes, and it is just this power which is the dignity of man ; and precisely in the unending exploration of science is its ennobling exhilaration. But who knows better than Faustus that progress in knowledge is good as well as evil ? He sells his soul for it ! And that enigmatic gesture, that piece of unmistakeably human behaviour—*that* is how the myth formulates the vague cloud of aspirations and suspicions, desires and disappointments, which I have just been attempting to formulate in terms of thought, as some sort of an idea. The myth makes no attempt to collect them into an idea ; suddenly, inexplicably, this mass of half-thought, half-feeling *lives* in our minds as the act of a man : Faustus sells his soul to the devil for some satisfaction of his lust to know. It is an act in which, inevitably, we recognize the virtue of a personality : it has only to be mentioned, to call up the man who was capable of it. And no less certainly we recognize the pressure of meaning behind the act.

Tragic Greatness : The Hero

The price of knowledge is damnation : and it is worth the price. No idea could concentrate its significance so deeply and intensely in us as this concrete symbolism, this moment in the life of a man ; and assuredly no idea could go home to us so instantly as this thrilling motion of characteristic human nature. The myth does not substantiate the person it supposes : there is little more personification in it than the single fact of the infernal bargain. But there is enough to make it apparent how the significance of the myth should work itself out in the logic of its personified symbolism. Suppose Faustus does somehow transcend the mere human version of things and acquire the immediacy of spiritual understanding. That is what we are to suppose by his *magic*. Yet what enterprise more desperate, more paradoxical, than for mortal intellect to aspire beyond mortality, only for its own mortal satisfaction ?—That is symbolized by Faust's damnation.

Of this symbolic figure, Marlowe made a living person—" human, all too human." When Faustus at last has the power for which he has bartered his soul, what does he do with it ? He plays tricks and japes ; he astonishes ostlers and courtiers, and annoys the Pope. And yet he is still the Faustus who could think of such a bargain : and the knowledge of his own self-contradiction, which is all he has gained by the power of his magic, turns his life into a fever worse than the desire of his youth, before the dreadful remedy of Mephistophilis allayed it. He becomes a delirium of passion for a phantom ; and it is time then for the devils to tear him to pieces—for Marlowe understands the logic of the mythical symbolism as well as how to please an Elizabethan audience.

Goethe added so much to this that he changed the whole sense of the story. The addition was gradual. In the first version of his tragedy he romanticized Faust's damnation by involving it with a love-affair. Vulgarization, compared with the single intensity of Marlowe's passion, obviously threatens. It was ingenious innovation, to shipwreck Faust in his ruin of Gretchen ; but what has this ordinary disaster to do with that terrible aspect of man's destiny which is represented by Faust's business with Mephistopheles ? It needs no formal

Tragic Greatness : The Hero

bargain with the devil to be a seducer of girls. Faust's transaction supposes an ambition more remarkable than that.

Did Goethe feel this ? His nature, at any rate, was, as he tells us himself, " too conciliating for tragedy." It seems, at first, an odd accommodation to such a nature, to make Faust survive Gretchen ; that, one would think, would rather be a fearful addition to his damnation. We accept it, however, first because this is now merely *Part I* of Goethe's whole intention ; secondly, because the story has otherwise been so modified, that even a love-affair now may justify itself in Faust's career. For the *Prologue in Heaven* has changed the sense of the legend. Faust is no longer the symbol of intellectual hunger alone. That may still predominate in him ; but he has become the stake in the eternal wager between good and evil ; and, very rightly. the ambition of his intellect has become the mere market or clearing-house of an ambition to have the whole possibility of life known and proved.

This is grandly carried out in *Part I* of Goethe's poem. Gretchen is no longer incongruous ; she is not even superfluous. She is a stage in Faust's career, and he has become a person capable of representing in his own experience the whole range of life's emotion. The contest of good and evil lives in our minds as the fortune of an astonishingly vivid character. But it is obviously incomplete. When Faust leaves Gretchen crazy in her cell, we know there is more to come. The wager is still undecided ; Mephistopheles, that brilliantly real emanation from the depth of Faust's desire, does not yet know whether he is to win or lose.

And the poem remains incomplete ; it fritters away in the anthology of wise remarks and the icy allegories of *Faust, Part II.* I do not forget the magical opening of this second part, nor its soaring conclusion. I can remember with admiration the Helena episode, with its marriage, if not of heaven and hell, at any rate of classicism and romanticism. And everyone respects the fifth act, with its justification of knowing not for itself, but as the means of doing. But what has happened to Faust all this while ? He has simply faded away, deserted by his author for tedious reflection and ungainly satire. The person of Faust has ceased to exist ; and so has his spirit of evil. *Faust, Part II,* is in its whole result a failure—and therefore the entire poem is a failure—because the personal symbol of it all has failed to go on living. Instead, we have a miscellany of notions. The incomparable legend of Faust has missed its artistic destiny. Twice it has become great poetry ; perhaps, remembering Lessing and Lenau, more than twice. But it has been frustrated in its effort to become supremely great, as it deserved to be. For when Marlowe endowed the myth with a consistent and impressively personal incarnation, the scope of its meaning was still too rigid ; and when Goethe gave it the required expansion, the figure in whose name this was done vanished out of it—the figure who was to have caught it all up into his potent being, and turned the whole of it into the living unity of a person. Faust himself had disappeared.

§ 3

Would it be unfair to contrast the second part of Goethe's *Faust* with one of Shakespeare's great tragedies ? That, at any rate, would be the way to realize what Goethe failed to accomplish. Who can mistake what it is that has issued out of Shakespeare's tragic art " conquering and to conquer " ? Everything that can contribute to greatness of poetry is there ; but what has taken possession of the world's imagination is the personal force of those figures into which the manifold art of his tragedy collects itself : Hamlet, Macbeth, Othello, Lear, and, in a slightly less degree, Coriolanus and Cleopatra. I say, the personal force of these figures : but in the force of each one of them lives a whole world of significance. In each of them, a sense of life, as profound and as unmistakeable as Goethe's, and governing at least as large a range of fortune and misfortune, has focussed the whole order of the process by which it became a poem into one vividly personal history. This was the habit of Shakespeare's tragic art ; and thus these presiding figures of his have a personal force which is indistinguishable from their symbolic force. I can only look at two of these figures ; but this will serve, besides illustrating still further our main topic, to show also how our idea of great poetry relates itself with the idea of tragedy. First, then, what is tragedy ?

This is a very old and a very formidable problem, this business of tragedy. We have been approaching it for some time : now it strides across our road, and we must face it. It is a giant notoriously disputatious and obstructive, and we had best avoid any altercation with him ; for we can hardly expect to skewer him once and for all with our answer to his riddle. But perhaps we can find an answer which will enable us, while he is thinking of a reply, to slip past him, and proceed to our conclusion.

For, after all, is tragedy anything more than a special case of the matters we have been discussing ? Poetry, we say, raises our experience of this world to the condition of ideal experience ; and that not by its expurgation of things, but by its subtly vibrant connexion of things. So that, in the perfection of this art—in a poem—whatever the matter may be, we live in a distinct system of connexion so thrilling and complete that everything there is relevant to everything else ; and the shapely order of our whole experience of this is an ideal experience, because everything in it, evil as well as good, is necessary to the *design of the whole.*

Now the peculiarity of tragedy is just this : it is, ostensibly, a version of the mere evil of life. The *design of the whole* here is man in disgrace and misfortune : the power of wickedness over virtue, the blind collaboration of events to destroy innocence, death frustrating love,—some aspect of the world in which this, or the like of this, so predominates, that everything else there is coloured by sorrow or pain. I say, it is ostensibly this : this is what analysis of the matter will show. But clearly something has escaped analysis, if this is its whole result. For tragedy is not merely sorrowful, not merely distressing : it is also and at the same time profoundly satisfactory. That could not be achieved by retribution of the evil, supposing there were occasion for it, and it suited the poet's purpose to take the occasion : for retribution (as for example, " poetic justice ") could only satisfy us *after* we had been distressed. But tragedy satisfies us even in the moment of distressing us. Satisfies ? The word is not strong enough. Tragedy does not exist unless it is *enjoyed*. Define it as you please ; but this, at any rate, is certain : if the notion of enjoyment does not somehow come in, you have failed to define tragedy at all, for you have left out a thing essential to its existence.

This is the real problem of tragedy : how do we come to enjoy what seems a version of the mere evil of life ? Nay, how is it that tragic art gives us the loftiest, though the severest, delight we can have in poetry ? It cannot simply be, because evil has become in it orderly and systematic. There might be a kind of maniacal æsthetic enjoyment in a vision of the world as an affair wholly organized for evil ; but that would be nothing like the enduring satisfaction which is the ground of tragic enjoyment. Indeed, there is no surer sign of a healthy mind than the enjoyment of tragedy. There must, then, be good as well as evil in it ; and out of the final harmony of the two, here, as elsewhere, will come the sense of the significance of evil overriding its injury—the sense that evil is no longer the intrusion of irresponsible and useless malignity, but the servant of universal law : which is the essence of the tragic satisfaction. Our æsthetic enjoyment of the spectacle of evil (which is certainly present in tragedy) is always accompanied by implicit assurance that we are not merely assisting at its triumph. But when we ask whence tragic poetry is to provide itself with good to match its evil, the answer can only be, that the good must arise out of the evil. This is what the peculiarity of tragedy comes to : out of things evil it must elicit good. That, you may remember, is what we found at the heart of Homer's valuation of life ; for, indeed, the tragic spirit descends to us from Homer, as Aristotle said. And now we can see why the tragic idealization of life has such a lofty delight for us : right in the very evil of life, in the thing most opposite to all our desires, even *there* experience has become desirable. May we not say, that man knows no height so superb above his mortal destiny as the art of tragedy—the height we live on when we assume the spirit of Æschylus or Sophocles, of Corneille or Racine, or of Shakespeare?

Tragic Greatness : The Hero

But I am not now to discuss tragedy in general, and the various methods (as those names suggest) by which its peculiar nature may be established ; I am only concerned with Shakespeare, and with him only in order to show how the method of his art falls in with our main argument.

Where, then, does Shakespeare's tragic art provide itself with good ? Precisely where all the evil of his tragedy concentrates and organizes itself ; and precisely also where we are to look for his final harmony of good and evil : in the *character* which creates and endures the evil. Out of him, whether he is blameworthy or not, goes the impulse which sets events conspiring against him ; and in the return it makes on him, the evil of the tragedy consists. It comes back to him with all the power it has collected in his world : the whole conspiracy enters into him and becomes incarnate in his personal life ; and thereby becomes evil : *his* evil, because it is his implacable enemy. He is the evil he endures ; and he is also the good which comes into being by reason of that evil, and his endurance of it. His personality drew destruction on itself ;

and in its resistance to destruction, in its assertion of itself against the hostility it has provoked—even though that assertion can be no more at last than exquisitely agonized perception of all the depth and subtlety of this enmity ;—in the heightening of the first of all the virtues, the virtue of personal existence ; in the white heat of man's most essential vigor, the vigor by which he is *himself against the world ;*—here it is that Shakespeare places the good his tragedy requires. It was this method of deriving good from evil (not peculiar to him, but by him most remarkably used) which enabled Shakespeare to be supreme in greatness of achievement above all other tragic poets ; for it enabled him to make tragedy of the utmost extremity of the evil of life, and to embody both the evil and the mastering of it in single personalities which have imposed themselves on the whole world's imagination. It enabled him, for example, to turn sordid motive and habitual crime into the tragedy of Macbeth ; and to make the whole of that tragedy consist in the life, the potently individual life, of its hero.

Macbeth starts off by bringing before us the very

powers of evil themselves, personified in figures of grisly vivacity, hideously blithe in their confidence of success : a confidence the more shocking because the witches, in that snatch of their infernal conversation with which the play opens, do not even allude to their hopes. It is merely their tone that instantly sets the key for all that is to follow. Ten lines of lyrical dialogue, and the action is in full career. No other play sweeps our imaginations at once into the full strength of its current like this.[1] From the very first word of it, we know, or at least feel, that the powers of evil are to have their will with the life of a man. Their temptation is the most devilish possible : what Macbeth dare not even desire is suddenly and awfully made to *appear* as the thing fated for him : all he has to do is to act accordingly.—Of course ! Once induce him to

[1] And in the most elaborate of recent editions of the play, this opening scene is set down as *spurious ;* expressly on the grounds that it is not *necessary :* " no dramatic interest or object is gained by its introduction," says this egregious editor, whose notions of dramatic interest are as scientific as his prosody— scientific, that is, only in the sense of being bluntly indifferent to art.

act, and the thing *is* thereby fated : it has been done !—All falls out as the witches prophesied. Macbeth acts, and has his ambition : but the witches did not tell him what he now finds out— that this is to descend alive into hell. Egged on by his wife, his first atrocious treachery, the murder of the king, gives him the vulgar aggrandizement he desires ; but a whole series of crimes must maintain it, each more futile than the last, each more patently ignoble in its motive. And when at last his own destruction stares at him, his life is not merely drencht in wickedness ; it has ceased to have any meaning ; it has become a phantasmagoria of horrible nonsense : a tale told by an idiot.

This is the process of evil in the tragedy : and it is wholly in Macbeth. The killing of Duncan, and the other murders, are evil in themselves, certainly ; but it is with the evil they are to Macbeth that the tragedy is concerned and our interest engaged. And not merely with the evil they are to Macbeth : the evil has become Macbeth himself, the very life of him. And in so doing it has provided itself with a perfect counterpart of good. For note how the two partners in crime react to their guilt. It is (with profound psychological truth) the hard calculating realist, the unimaginative matter-of-fact businesslike instigator—it is Lady Macbeth, who shatters and gives in to the strain of horror and danger she has brought upon herself. But Macbeth goes on enduring to the last: the sensitive highly-strung Macbeth, the fearfully imaginative man, who can see the whole infamy of his crime as soon as he has thought of it, and anticipates all the possibility of its failure ; the man who sees visionary emblems of intended crime and the ghosts of crime committed, as clearly as if they were commonplace reality ; the man who instantly translates the witches' greeting into the thought of murder, instantly begins devising, has it all complete in his mind, and then has to be forced on to do the thing he has pledged himself to do : and as he goes out on his hideous business, looks on at himself, as if he were watching a figure in a drama, moving " with Tarquin's ravishing strides " towards his victim, while he feels the very earth he treads on repudiate its complicity : this is the person who stands up to the end, who grandly looks despair in the face, and dies fighting, unsubdued. It is not merely that he becomes more daring and resolute in action, the more desperate his affairs become : the whole vitality of the man becomes incandescent. Infinitely keener than Lady Macbeth's is his suffering ; and the more he suffers, the more capable of suffering he becomes ; and the more he steels himself to endure : *that* is what the singular ability of his personal life has become. And when Lady Macbeth dies, and he realizes that he is alone in the dreadful world he has created for himself, the unspeakable abyss suddenly opens beneath him. He has staked everything and lost ; he has damned himself for nothing ; his world suddenly turns into a blank of imbecile futility. And he seizes on the appalling moment and masters even this : he masters it by *knowing* it absolutely and completely, and by forcing even this quint-essence of all possible evil to live before him with the zest and terrible splendor of his own unquench-able mind :

Tragic Greatness : The Hero

> To-morrow, and to-morrow, and to-morrow,
> Creeps in this petty pace from day to day
> To the last syllable of recorded time,
> And all our yesterdays have lighted fools
> The way to dusty death. Out, out, brief candle !
> Life's but a walking shadow, a poor player
> That struts and frets his hour upon the stage
> And then is heard no more : it is a tale
> Told by an idiot, full of sound and fury,
> Signifying nothing.

There is no depth below that ; that is the bottom. Tragedy can lay hold of no evil worse than the conviction that life is an affair of absolute inconsequence. There is no meaning anywhere : that is the final disaster ; death is nothing after that. And precisely by laying hold of this and relishing its fearfulness to the utmost, Macbeth's personality towers into its loftiest grandeur. Misfortune and personality have been until this a continual discord : but now each has reached its perfection, and they unite. And the whole tragic action which is thus incarnate in the life of Macbeth—what is it but the very polar opposite to the thing he proclaims ? For we see not only what he feels, but the personality that feels it ; and in the very act of proclaiming that life is " a tale told by an idiot, *signifying nothing*," personal life announces its virtue, and superbly *signifies itself*. That, so far as it can be reduced to abstract words, is the action of *Macbeth*. But it is no abstract meaning, but the poem as an actual whole, that lives in our minds : *there* is the shapely order and intense connexion of things that can absorb even Macbeth's " tale told by an idiot" in the sense of a final significance. And what is this significance ? Nothing but the completely organized and focussed unity of the poem's total impression ; and that is nothing but the figure and person of Macbeth himself : in him the whole poem lives and has its meaning. In his un-analysable quality as an individual we recognize a symbol of life itself, creating and enduring—yes, and dreadfully relishing—its own tragic destiny.

I have taken *Macbeth* as the type of Shakespeare's method in tragedy ; and we see how the success of that method has made *Macbeth* a type also of the poetry which the world acknowledges as supremely great—the poetry which collects itself into figures unique in personal force and universal in significance. If there is any such figure more famous than Macbeth, it is Hamlet ; but I can only glance at him. Macbeth's tragedy is in the failure of his world : it could not have been avoided, and his agonized triumph over it lasts but a moment. But Hamlet has to face the failure of himself ; it is an affair dreadfully prolonged, and he is always telling himself that it might have been avoided—if he had not been Hamlet ! Macbeth suffers a metaphysical disaster, Hamlet a psychological disaster ; and the latter, no doubt, is the more familiar to our sympathies. Nowadays, at any rate, where metaphysic claims its hundreds, psychology claims its tens of thousands.

What is this disaster, then ? We see Hamlet as he sees himself ; and we also see him as the living harmony of an immense complexity of events. Everyone knows how Hamlet sees himself :

> I do not know
> Why yet I live to say " this thing's to do."

He bitterly despises himself for his failure to act :

he can but think and talk about acting, and return again and again to his self-contempt. And the critics, innocently taking him at his own valuation, have held him up to reprobation as the man who could not kill his uncle. He is, they say, the very figure of moral vacillation : and Hamlet himself agrees with them.

This hardly accounts for his extraordinary prestige : it is certainly not as a contemptible figure that Hamlet has impressed the world. What no one can mistake, at any rate, is the fact that he is very vividly alive : he has that inexplicably individual force which is the essence of personality, and which can make itself consistently felt through all the contradictions of thought and action—contradictions, which, because of that unique force inspiring them, we always feel to be, as we say, *in character*. It is a force for which no formula can ever be found ; any attempt to describe it will leave out something vital. But it is odd that the critics, in their attempts to describe Hamlet's personality, should have so often left out that most unmistakeable, though certainly very indefinable, thing, his heroism.

Tragic Greatness : The Hero

Very indefinable indeed, someone will say : the heroism of moral vacillation ! Well, let us look at this vacillation a little ; and as I said just now, we must see it not merely as it appears to Hamlet himself, but as it appears in the play as a whole. Hamlet, we may agree, has made up his mind that he ought to kill the king. That has not been an easy decision to arrive at. He might very well *want* to kill Claudius : he has terrible motives for hating him. But such a decision must have not merely desire, but a conviction of duty, at the back of it. Hamlet knows well enough that desire is easily mistaken for duty. But his long anguish of self-contempt would be without meaning, unless he were convinced that justice, as well as his own desire, demanded the death of Claudius : he must, that is, be convinced that Claudius killed his father. The evidence for that is, to say the least, very dubious : the eloquence of a ghost, and the king's behaviour at the play. Either might be explained away, as Hamlet can see. They certainly do not form a body of evidence on which the king might be publicly impeacht. Still, Hamlet at length is convinced, though by a somewhat insecure and uneasy process : he feels, rather than knows, the king's guilt : a species of conviction which he cannot share with anyone. The king must die, however ; even though Hamlet can have nothing to rely on but his own ingenuity, and assassination plots in palaces are not lightly brought off. He makes a beginning by feigning madness : but he gets no further. What else ought he to have done ?

Anything, say the moralists, rather than deplore his own faculty for delaying action. But they can say nothing so contemptuous of his pitiable introspection as what Hamlet says himself. And what of the play all this while ? What *are* these delays which Hamlet so loathes himself for making, or, at least, allowing ? As the action unfolds itself, we watch Hamlet continually upbraiding himself for delay which—simply does not exist ! There is no delay at all : there is no moment in the play in which we see Hamlet failing to kill the king, no moment of which he could have taken any conceivable advantage, except that single one in which he catches the king at his prayers : a moment which he rejects precisely because it is the *wrong* moment for his revenge—it is too favorable to the king's hereafter. Those contemptible delays, those moral vacillations, for which Hamlet is so notorious, exist wholly in Hamlet's own mind. They are, for him, none the less real and disastrous. They form the tragic harmony of his personal life and the events to which it belongs : none other was possible.

Hamlet, already deeply injured in his emotions by his mother's indecent marriage, becomes possessed by a terrible desire, which must be, to his wounded mind, as corrosive as vitriol, unless he can get rid of it. And it is not a mere personal craving, this desire ; it is the thing in which he has come profoundly to believe : the thing, he says, that ought to happen, that must happen. And this desire, as a matter of practical fact, never has a chance of happening. Eventually, it might have found or made its opportunity ; but as long as Hamlet knows it, circumstances are adamant against it. Indeed, it is a desire that could only proceed into action most gradually and delicately : but its possessor cannot meanwhile endure to nurse it privately as the mere inaction of desire. The whole world is out of tune while it remains ineffective : for it is justice, this desire. *Why* is justice less able than the brute process of events ? There must be some reason ! And the baffled desire returns upon its possessor, and curdles his life, " like eager droppings into milk " ; it becomes his poison, and his poisoned life looks in on itself, and knows itself incurably vitiated by the fierce desire it can never get rid of. The poisoned introspection of a noble mind hates itself and despises itself. The fearful conclusion leaps at him. *He himself* is the reason why his desire remains unacted : he is *unworthy* of it. Justice would have been done, had not his cowardice *delayed* it ! This is the famous delay we hear about in Hamlet's soliloquies ; it is the tragic invention of his own wounded mind.

I have nothing to say of the inferiority complex ; I will only remind you that as long ago as Homer's *Odyssey* a character exactly similar to Hamlet took its place in literature. I mean the character of Telemachus. In him we see a desire, a just and noble desire, which is, by the very nature of things, unable to realize itself in action. Events are not merely unfavourable to it : it never has the least chance of insinuating itself into the actuality of events. It can only be thought about, and cherisht in day-dreams. And it turns back on itself, detesting its own futility ; and becomes its possessor's self-contempt and self-loathing. And that is the profound significance of Hamlet : that is what gives him his prestige, as an individual person capable of representing human nature itself. He is the most unflinching exposure that has ever been made of the trapt anguish of human nature when it finds itself pitifully weaker than events ; but in Hamlet it is a weakness inextricably involved with human nature's finest strength. As usual in Shakespeare, the tragedy of the events consists wholly in their transformation into the very stuff of the personal life around which they organize themselves. The *evil* of Hamlet's tragedy is that the only harmony he can find, to resolve the discord of what he desires and what is possible, is bitter self-contempt. But the harmony *we*, the onlookers, find is in that same character's concentration of the whole order of the poem into itself; and how can we find harmony there unless we can find good there to match the evil? But who can miss the good in Hamlet's character? For it is a character which can keep its distinction, even in the midst of its horrible secret disaster: which can be nice and courteous, kindly and amiable, wittily fastidious and greatly indignant, urbanely ironical and serenely disillusioned, even when it privately despises and detests the very nature of its own existence. That is the *good* of Hamlet's tragedy: and heroism is not too strong a word for it. It is, perhaps, a stouter heroism even than Macbeth's.

LECTURE V

POETIC PERSONALITY. THE POET HIMSELF

§ 1

I HAVE never professed, in these lectures, to make great poetry into a *species* of poetry. There are, as I have said, infinite degrees of greatness ; if we could set up any kind of a scale for poetry in respect of it, we should never be able to mark exactly where greatness begins, any more than we can draw the line on the thermometer where *heat* begins. But put your hand into hot water, and you know it is hot, right enough ; enter into great poetry, and you feel, just as unmistakeably, the greatness. The analysis of this feeling which I have been attempting has been designed to show that we can, nevertheless, say with some precision what it is we are acknowledging when we admit the greatness of poetry ; and that, in consequence, we can also say, without pretending to anything so futile as a nice measurement of greatness, why

The Idea of Great Poetry

some poems strike us as greater than others. Poetry being always a harmony of experience, its greatness will depend both on the scope and variety of the experience, and on the completeness and intensity of the harmony of this. *Prometheus Unbound* is not so great a poem as *Paradise Lost*, because the experience Shelley made into his poem has neither the scope nor the variety of Milton's. But neither is *Faust* as great a poem as *Paradise Lost*, though the range of Goethe's matter is not unequal to, and not altogether unlike, Milton's ; the thing here is, that Goethe could effect nothing like Milton's harmony. For Milton centred his harmony deep in the peculiarly personal life of a character ; Goethe's harmony began as a character, slackened into the easier harmony of an idea, and then dissipated into the mere juxtaposition of variety.

There are some poems which the world seems agreed to place in a class above all others, so far as greatness is concerned. They may not be above all others in the scope of their experience—not decisively, at any rate ; for once that can be taken as fairly and fully representative of the whole fact

Poetic Personality

of life, its sorrow and its joy, its power and its ruin, we have reached a height which will not be notably affected by more or less detail in the substantiation. There is still, however, the possibility of a further and decisive step upward towards supreme greatness ; and we found that this step upward is taken when the poet's art raises the harmony of its matter to the highest degree of command and intensity, by making it live in our minds as the personality of a character manifestly symbolic—a Satan, an Achilles, a Hamlet. We saw also why this personified harmony must have such a superiority of command over our minds and such an intensity of concentration. For no mere idea can excite us so profoundly or draw us to live in it so keenly, as the fortune of a character whose similarity to ourselves cannot but provoke our sympathy ; and there can be no such unification of diversity—yes, and of opposites and contradictions—as that mysterious, not-to-be-formulated power of personality can effect, simply by uttering these diverse things out of the depth of its fund of nameless power, and thereby charging them all, however they may differ, with the unique savor of its quality : thus giving us underneath our sense of diversity, and even of contradiction, a still deeper sense of connexion—the sense, namely, of an originating personal life.

But so far I have simply taken for granted the fact of this symbolic characterization. How a poet can create an imaginary character in our minds— and a character which is not only absolutely in- dividual but at the same time a symbol of the poet's intention—is a question we should, perhaps, leave to the psychologists. Is it due to the poet's observation of life ? But observation will not give us a Macbeth, any more than a Satan. Is it then the poet expressing himself ? But Milton is not Satan ; and if Shakespeare is Macbeth, how can he be also his other characters—Cleopatra and Benedick, Isabella and Prospero ? We find a similar problem in the art of landskip. If it is merely observation, it is nothing ; but, in the nature of it, it is something else than the artist himself. If we cannot expect to meet with Falstaffs and Hamlets in actual life, neither can we expect to see in the open air what Turner or Crome put on canvas : the artist is there, as well as the scene of the earth.

So with poetic characterization. The poet has lived in the world of men, and has come to know that world through and through, delighting in it. But his observation comes to us completely impregnated by his peculiar spirit and by the purpose of his art. Observation will never account for creation ; it will not even account for the materials of creation, unless we take it in a sense large enough to include introspection. Milton is neither Satan nor Christ ; but it was almost wholly on his knowledge of himself that he drew for the materials out of which he created the characters of Satan and Christ. It may, indeed, be said, and justly, that observation itself is always in some sort creative ; for it does not merely consist in noticing traits of behaviour, it goes on to the distinctly imaginative act, not merely of *combining* them (which would be nothing), but of *supposing* a character capable of *producing* such behaviour. Even so, this imaginative character-drawing which we call observation of life is conditioned solely by what we know. The poet's character-drawing, however, is conditioned not only by what he knows, but also by what he requires—for the accomplishment of an artistic purpose to which all his characterization is subordinate. Realism is not the standard by which we can judge of his success ; and when we say that his characters are *true to life*, all we mean is that they are *intelligible*. And intelligible they must be, if they are to serve his purpose ; they must be characters into whose thoughts and moods and actions we can readily enter, and feel them as our own. But if they are intelligible, we do not trouble to ask whether they are true to life in the realistic sense ; we are not disturbed by the fact that every moment of their speech and language is distinctly significant—a thing we scarcely find in the persons of actual life : nor that these imaginary characters, as if it was the most natural thing in the world, continually reveal the very inmost secrets of their beings and their deep reaction to the events and persons round about them : nor—and this is equally unlike what actually happens—that they are presented to us absolutely and wholly conditioned by one single process of things, altogether concerned in that and in that only. In a word, our belief in these characters is not in the least affected by the fact that they, their thoughts and feelings and personalities, are as much the expressive technique of the poet's purpose as his phrases and his rhythms.

But what do we mean by the *personality* of a fictitious character ? What gives us the sense of a personality existing in its own right—and not merely the poet's—in an imaginary spectacle of human behaviour ? The poet, we must remember, is severely limited in the means of his art ; he works, moreover, under the strict self-imposed conditions of his artistic purpose ; and yet he compels us to imagine a series of thoughts, feelings, actions, in such a way that an individual person, and an apparently independent person, comes into life within them, as convincingly as if he had actually lived before us with all the freedom and infinite subtlety of real acquaintance. How is it done ? We talk, rather portentously, of *analysis* and *psychology* in poetry. But these are rarities—I might say, oddities—in poetry. Indeed, I know

The Idea of Great Poetry

of only one genuinely psychological poem—that amazing and, to me, thrilling thing, *Peter Bell*. Where else does poetry concern itself with *the way the mind works*? Except in such a *bravura*-piece as *Peter Bell*, what the poets are interested in, when they portray human nature, is *the result of a mind's working*. And this must be so. It is necessary to their purpose to make their characters, as far as possible, proclaim themselves ; this is true of epic as well as of dramatic poetry ; for it is the only way these characters can be made to come to life in us in their own unmistakeable style. And that must be done intelligibly : that is to say, these characters must live in the same sort of consciousness in which we ourselves live. But what is it we are conscious of ? Of our thoughts and our moods ; but not of the obscurely conflicting forces which make our minds what they are, not of the mystery out of which these thoughts and moods emerge. That mystery is what Wordsworth was concerned with in *Peter Bell ;* and it is the topic of psychology. The core of the topic is personality ; and the method of its science is analysis. But the method

Poetic Personality

of poetry is not analysis : it is exhibition. Poetry, even when we can speak of its revelation of the inmost secrecies of a character, is still showing us *what* a mind has produced, not *how* this mind has produced it.

Perhaps an analogy, rough as it must be, will make this clearer. We are watching, let us suppose, a tarn in a pocket of the hills ; we are noting the play of the breezes on the surface of the waters. The curves of the rippling pattern are enough to engage our attention. Unless we are very determined scientists, we do not trouble to think of, much less think out, the complicated dynamics of the moving airs which that ripple results from. We could draw, if we had the right skill, the effect of wind on water ; and I daresay also, if again we had the right skill, we could make out the mathematical equations of the forces in the air and their friction on the water. Well : there is no more similarity between the poet's and the psychologist's account of character than there is between a picture of ruffled water and the mathematics of its cause. In a *tour de force*, one might make poetry of mathematics ; in a *tour de force*, poetry has been made of psychology—in *Peter Bell*.

But normally poetry simply exhibits *behaviour*, whether inner or outer : not trying to account for those forces which make their appearance in behaviour, as breezes make their appearance in troubled water. Yet, if we truly portray the trouble of the water, we give the sense of invisible wind by its effect on that which is, in all its motions, visible. Just so the poet in his exhibition of human behaviour must convey the sense of that which cannot be exhibited—personality. Once more, how is it done ? How does a colossal, a superhuman character, a Satan or a Prometheus, to say nothing of a Macbeth or an Achilles, become credible to us as a personality, even though its symbolic function must live in it as clearly as its individual force ?

I put these questions more for the purpose of showing where their solution lies, than of solving them. Up to a point, it is not difficult to see how the sense of a *personality* may emerge out of a mass of *characterization :* for the two are by no means identical. Who does not know how common it is

Poetic Personality

in literature, to have elaborate characterization which never begins to impress us as the authentic life of a person ? Yet how simply and obviously the great poets seem to effect that impression ! They bring in, perhaps, some sharply individualizing trait ; and with one stroke the character has personality in him. Richard Crookback, the man born to " snarl and bite and play the dog," has no grudge against his own deformity : on the contrary, he is quite good-natured about it ; he is actually amused at it. This is much more convincing than the obvious thing. If he had railed at it, we should have accepted that as very natural ; that is what we might have expected, and it would have given him a very possible character. But the malignant who can quite genuinely see and enjoy nature's joke against him—that is not only a character : that is a person. Such traits are the better in effect the more they are unexpected. One of the best in the world is the rejection of Falstaff by his beloved Prince Hal. At last Falstaff's great moment has come ; his prince is on his way to be crowned King of England ; and—" I know thee not, old man!" That is the end of Falstaff, the most loveable, and certainly one of the most admirable, of immortal men: " Master Shallow, I owe you a thousand pound." And it is the beginning of Henry as a person—an admirable, but not a very loveable person. Who has not been shockt by this catastrophe of all Falstaff's hopes? No dramatic surprise could be more complete; none more convincing.[1] Instantly, what has hitherto been the mere characterization of Henry becomes the inexplicable, the irresistible force of a person: now we know just *who* it is that has been so long sharing in Falstaff's disreputable gusto. He is the man who can steep himself in wickedness because he knows that nothing can soil him. He can touch pitch and not be defiled: the filth of the world has no more power over his mind than dust has to

---

[1] The catastrophe has, indeed, been prepared: there have been clear hints that something of this kind was like to happen. But it is safe to say that no one, on a first reading, was ever prepared for it to happen in this manner. It is the manner of it that is so shocking, and so convincing. It reveals Henry to us as formidably as Odysseus was revealed to the suitors when he stript off his rags and shot Antinoos.

Poetic Personality

sully white-hot iron. This is the man to succeed in the world : this is the *person* inside that dazzling behaviour called Harry the Fift.

The man is more than his actions. However much of his character is shown us—doing, thinking, feeling or what not—that is not all ; something still lies behind : for all this comes out of an inexhaustible, incalculable fund of spiritual energy : and all, however contradictory it may seem, has its unity and its origin out of this deeply concealed yet unmistakeably divined source. That is what it is to feel *personality* within, behind, and always informing, *character*. If it does convince us at all, it convinces us the more, the more inexplicable it is. For personality is not a thing we can explain ; and to feel it most, that is the quality of it we must feel the most. When Richard woos and wins the Lady Anne, his preposterous success is the very thing on which we base our belief in his personality : for what else could succeed in this style but sheer personal force ? But the deepest sense of personality springs from something much less localized and definitely characteristic than this. Who can explain our love for Falstaff ? He does nothing we do not know we ought to reprobate ; and he does nothing we do not love him for doing. And when virtue at last rejects him, all our feelings side with him against virtue. Why ? There is no rational answer ; throughout the whole of his characterization, his personality irrationally shows, infinitely transcending all the manner of its appearance, and quite unmistakeable. It is the person we love, let the character—the manifestation of the person—be what it will.

In fact, the distinctly appreciable moments, in which the soul of personality shines through its vesture of character, would seldom make their effect unless the personal force we there so noticeably feel had been implicit throughout. When Satan, in that magnificent moment at the beginning of his enterprise against man's innocence, is suddenly seized by a desire to repent, in his appalled realization of the doom he has brought on himself ; and then grandly recovers the only secure mood for him : we feel that the symbolic behaviour of a character has become, as it were, transparent, and we see through the character into the depths of a personality:

> Me miserable ! Which way shall I flie
> Infinite wrauth, and infinite despaire ?
> Which way I flie is Hell ; my self am Hell ;
> And in the lowest deep a lower deep
> Still threatning to devour me opens wide. . . .
> So farwel Hope, and with Hope farwel Fear,
> Farwel Remorse : all Good to me is lost ;
> Evil be thou my Good. . . .

Yet the possibility of this prodigious moment of tragic emotion has been implicit in Satan from the start. He has been throughout a character symbolizing a paradox, the pride of individual rebellion against almighty destiny, the very figure of the absolute antinomy—fixt fate, free will. Now this antinomy appears as something more than the behaviour we watch or the character we understand ; it comes on us now with irresistible inexplicable certainty as the very life of personal being. But what we have now, only confirms what we hitherto could but feel : the character could scarcely have lived in our minds at all unless we had been able to feel what we can now see so clearly.

The Idea of Great Poetry

Obviously, then, it will not do simply to compound, however skilfully, the ingredients of a character, if we are to feel the life of the person out of which character emerges. The personality must have been living in the poet's mind, with perfect distinction of its unique and unaccountable quality, before he committed it to his art ; and the pressure of its personal quality makes itself felt in the poet's technique by an infinity of minute strokes of which he himself, probably, is hardly aware, and which no critical analysis will ever quite reckon up. The real problem is, then, how a poet's purpose can transform itself in his mind into the form and the authority of a living independent personality. I can do no more than indicate the place of the problem in that mystery of *how the mind works*, which poetry willingly leaves to psychology.

And the problem lies deep in that mystery, possibly below the reach of rational apprehension. Once more, analogy may help us to understand its nature. An exactly similar problem meets us in the case of that kind of imagery which is called *apocalyptic*. Swedenborg is the classic instance.

202

Poetic Personality

He lived in visions which presented themselves to his mind vividly and involuntarily ; but, however fantastically irresponsible they might seem, they always had a meaning for him. There was always what he darkly called some " correspondence " in them. His conscious mind, by means of them, was telling itself of things that had taken place profoundly underneath its consciousness : they were the pattern of ripples in his mind produced by an incalculable wind. The most he could do towards understanding them was to infer the presence of the wind of the spirit, and something of its direction. Thus, Swedenborg sees some clergy entering heaven : " as they ascended together, they appeared at a distance like calves. On their entrance into heaven they were received with civility by the angels, but when they conversed with them, they were seized with trembling, afterwards with horror, and at last as if with the agonies of death, upon which they cast themselves headlong, and in their descent they appeared like dead horses." The " correspondence " of this is as surprising as the imagery ; for " from correspondence the understanding of truth has the appearance of a horse, and the non-understanding of truth that of a dead horse." Understanding of truth—non-understanding of truth—what does that mean ? Who knows ? Certainly not Swedenborg ; the terms are but his labels for obscure disturbances in the depths of his being. But he has seen these disturbances take visible form in his mind—form unaccountable, and yet charged with importance : he has seen the horses and the dead horses which are to him symbolic.

But we do not have to be Swedenborgs, nor mystical eccentrics of any kind, in order to experience the imagery which is lived in as something charged with " correspondence." We need be merely what everyone must be at one time or another—*dreamers*. Something happens to us, or within us, while we are asleep. We do not know what is happening ; but it is presented to us in an involuntary symbolism, it is translated into a train of imagery, an experience of events as clear as anything actual can be, and instinct with singular importance. Knocking on the door, for example, becomes an adventure with demons in a thundering factory. The insistent summons, joined by an ambush of lurking emotions, is something our sleeping consciousness can only know as the inexplicable air of *meaning* which the vision of the dream carries with it. And just so works the mind of a poet when a mass of profoundly obscure disturbance is presented to his mind in the figure of a personality unaccountably and vividly alive, yet charged with symbolic significance : such a personality, for example, as the Prometheus of Æschylus. What was it which the power, known to most of us only in dreams, presented to Æschylus' mind as the sublime behaviour and person of Prometheus ? I necessarily give it the spurious definition of *thought :* it was not thought, but indefinable spiritual energy, which dramatized itself in the figure of the crucified Titan. It was something of this kind.

Man is in the current of a divinely implacable destiny ; but he is made of free will, and he can only live by asserting his will against his destiny, which is the power of God. God resents this and will avenge it. Progress is evil and to be punished. To God the force of the world is just because it is

The Idea of Great Poetry

His own; to man it must be unjust because it is against him. And as destiny must accept man's will, but will nevertheless punish it; so man's will must accept destiny, but is nevertheless unconquerable. And as the triumphant force of the world belongs to a god of immitigable justice, so the passion of man's life becomes an opposite god of unmerited suffering. Only as gods can both justice and injustice be endured : and both must be endured. But it is intelligence, and not strength, which will rule in the long run.

If this is not guessed aright, it was at any rate something of this nature; probably the elements were vaguer, more massively intangible, more mutually incompatible, and also much more insistent.

What, for example, I have put down as " Progress is evil," would more likely be a shadowy relic of loyalty to the tribe—the vague and infinitely serious feeling that, since the only safety is the tribe, everything new is unsafe, since it may loosen or at least unsettle the elaborately strict complexity of tribal society : and the rest of my hypothetical statement could be similarly expanded.

Poetic Personality

How could such a congeries ever be imagined in that unity of experience which alone can inspire a poem ? Not by any intellectual organization, but by some irrational process of fusion that could only occur in the unconscious depth of the poet's being, precisely on the analogy of a dream. But this having occurred, the life of it could only be known—again on the analogy of a dream—in some kind of involuntary dramatization, an image inexplicably symbolizing its origin. The poet's useful possession of this power in his waking hours, as well as in the useless fantasies of sleep, is one of the privileges of what we call genius ; and if he is a great poet, and the impulses stirring in him are vigorous and important enough, the dramatic symbolism whereby his mind presents to him their obscure unification will be not merely the spectacle and behaviour of human character, but the distinct energy of a person. This is not a phenomenon of the ages of mythology only. Precisely the same process which gave Æschylus his Prometheus gave, to add modern instances to those already mentioned, Ibsen his Brand and Nietzsche his Zarathustra. Was it

207

not also a mere modification of this process which enabled Walt Whitman to create, out of the wealth of his noble experience, that vividly personal figure which is surely one of the few supremely great things in modern poetry—the figure of himself? But of this kind of symbolic personality there is an instance even more remarkable, which may well be taken as its type ; and with some account of this, my argument must conclude.

§ 2

The things which seem to us most inevitable are, for that very reason, as soon as we begin to look into them, the most mysterious things. Nothing could seem more inevitable than the imaginary personalities in which the power of the greatest poetry lives. Far from trying to explain them, I have been endeavouring to show how mysterious they are : and I have been fortunate indeed if I have succeeded merely in making it plain what the mystery is, which lies behind not only Prometheus and his analogues—Job, Satan, Faustus—but also behind Hamlet and Macbeth, Achilles and Hector :

Poetic Personality

behind any character which lives in our minds both as unique personality, and also as poetic technique— the symbolic expression of the poet's sense of the significance of things.

Any such character may be the means of the supremely great in poetry : his large symbolic virtue is the scope, and the intensifying virtue of his personality is the harmony, which we require for poetic greatness : the harmony, namely, which comes of the issue of everything the symbolism includes or can suggest out of a single fund of energy, imagined as a personal existence. But are such characters as those I have just named the only kind of personified harmony ? Are they the only ones to be reckoned with, in our account of what the world has accepted as great, and supremely great, in poetry ? That can hardly be : for reflect only, that we have not yet taken account of Lucretius and Dante. If they are not great, and supremely great, poets, who is ? There is still, therefore, something to be said : we have still to consider the poetry in which the greatness lives in the symbolic personality of the *poet himself*. I will take Dante as the type of this ; and it would not be difficult to justify the choice of him rather than of Lucretius. I could never sufficiently express my admiration for Lucretius ; and his motives command my sympathies more than Dante's can ever do. But Dante the theological man is the focus of a far larger, though perhaps not deeper, experience than Lucretius the intellectual man ; and assuredly Dante's personality is the more potent and imposing of the two. Do I, by taking Dante's achievement last, mean to suggest that it is the greatest of those which I have discussed ? That is possible. It is at any rate certain that the pyramid of poetic qualities, narrowing as they rise until we stand on the apex of supremely great achievement, is nowhere so clear as in the poetry of Dante : I mean, of course, in his *Divine Comedy*.

But have we not already had the poet who expresses himself ? Wordsworth and Leopardi, for instance, have their ideas of life ; but is not our real interest directed, by means of these ideas, on the personal life of the poets themselves ? That is partly true, no doubt : though not, of course,

Poetic Personality

in the sense that we require biography in order to appreciate, or even to improve our appreciation of, these poets. But however true it may be, we yet merely *infer*, as best we may, the personalities behind the poems, with no assurance either of completeness of knowledge or even of certainty in it. No such inference is needed in the case of the poets of whom I take Dante as the grand type. These poets create in their works the figure of their own personal lives as certainly as Shakespeare creates Hamlet or Milton creates Satan ; and they do it in precisely the same manner—not by *truth to life* in the realistic sense, but by concentration and enhancement. Every moment of the vitality they portray is intensely significant of the peculiar personality behind it ; and it is a personality which reveals the inmost motion of its being to our delighted and assured clairvoyance ; and finally it is a personality of which the impression is complete and whole—a *unity* of personal life. In a word, it is a personality poetically created ; and created for a poetical purpose. It is the focus of the matter, and the governance of the form, of the poem. In the manner of the life it assumes in our imaginations, the poet has made a symbol of his purpose ; and there is really, at the back of this impersonation of a poet's sense of life, the same mystery which we have found in the case of such objective characters as Prometheus or Macbeth.

Whether Lucretius or Dante would have admitted this central concern of their art with their own personal lives is a question scarcely pertinent. I have no doubt Lucretius would have said his theme was the philosophy of Epicurus ; Dante might have said his theme was Holy Church revealing the destiny of man. The fact remains that the poetic symbol of Epicurus' philosophy is the majestic intellectual experience of Lucretius himself—an intellectual experience always charged with the force of a unique and noble personality : and a symbol, moreover, not merely of a particular philosophy, but of the whole sublime ambition of human intellect : namely, to conceive the sum of experience as a rational harmony. And as for Dante—but that is what must now engage my endeavours.

There are many recognized indications of insanity :

Poetic Personality

none more reliable, I suppose, than the conviction of having something new to say about Dante. You will not, I hope, think I am qualifying for the attentions of the alienists now. What I have to say about *The Divine Comedy* is not offered as anything new, but simply in the interests of my argument, which would be left flagrantly incomplete without some notice of that astonishing poem. It is obvious, from what has been said, that *The Divine Comedy* can only be taken as an instance of greatness in poetry, if it is taken in its quality *as a whole*. It happens that this quality has been denied the right to any poetic existence at all by the most eminent of living critics, the man to whom æsthetic theory owes a quite incalculable debt, Benedetto Croce. There would be some excuse, therefore, for considering afresh at least one aspect of Dante's achievement, apart from the fact that it is the aspect our topic requires us to consider. We must face and, if we can, counter the notion, that it is not *The Divine Comedy* as a whole which is poetry, but merely certain moments and episodes in it : the so-called poem as a whole being really a " theological novel," which has poetic merit only in so far as it provides fitting occasions for poetry—that is, for momentary poetry. In that case, not only is *The Divine Comedy* not great as poetry (however great it may be as a monument of theology at a certain stage), but there is no such thing as poetic greatness at all, in the sense these lectures have been supposing.

We shall certainly not disagree with Croce and his followers in their estimate of the momentary poetry of *The Divine Comedy*. We cannot admire it enough ; yet even so we may admire it chiefly as the means whereby the poem as a whole comes into existence, as successive layers building up the pyramid of supreme poetic greatness. I merely allude therefore, in the most cursory manner possible, to those qualities for which Dante is, no doubt, most easily praised ; for my concern is with that poetic achievement which exists, if it exists at all, as superstructure resting on these.

No greater mastery of words has ever been shown than in *The Divine Comedy ;* and I think it would be safe to say of some parts of *Paradiso*, that such an *incantation* as Dante there effects out

Poetic Personality

of the sound and meaning of language can nowhere else be found. Words take on a new being in Dante's poetry: they have more force and more delicacy of force than we could ever have suspected. He is the standing example of the First Law of Poetics, that the greater the inspiration, the more art is required. Such fierce pressure of personal life as Dante's, such white-hot condensation of manifold experience into instantaneous self-consciousness, could never have reacht our minds without the skill which can use with miraculous precision every possible power of language in simultaneous complexity of effect. And it is interesting to compare the subtle faculty of suggestion which his early poetry has, with the complete domination he can exert over us in *The Divine Comedy*. No poet takes such absolute possession of our minds as he does there.

But as to what he does with this masterful enchantment of our minds, there is no end to the praise of that. I mention only those things which obviously serve to build up our pyramid towards its apex. We may note first the air of sharp lucid

The Idea of Great Poetry

realism which he makes his imaginary experience
assume : as, for example, in those many strokes
which bring home to us the living man alone among
ghosts : only he can cast a shadow in this spectral
world, and his disembodied companions are amazed
to see once more that familiar sign of earthly life ;
only he, when he is to be ferried across the Styx,
makes the boat dip in the water as he steps
aboard. This is the power, too, which, in a few
lines, brands upon our memories the living attitude
and inmost personal force of such figures as
Francesca, Ulysses, Sordello ; and which makes
the progress of the poem a series of unforgettably
impressive and minutely precise incidents. I merely
hazard one or two specimens : the indifferent angel
who comes down to hell to give orders to the furies,
walking over Styx " con le piante asciutte," and
waving away the foul air,

menando la sinistra innanzi spesso ;

the grotesque solemnity of the escort of demons,
and their suddenly flaring quarrel ; the descent
of the two angels in Antipurgatorio, and the blinding
beauty of their faces ; " Casella mio " and his song,

che la dolcezza ancor dentro mi suona ;

Poetic Personality

Filippo Argenti, " pien di fango," and Dante's immortal hatred :

>   con piangere e con lutto,
> Spirito maladetto, ti rimani !

Still more astonishing are those unaccountable visions, which we are made to see as distinctly as if we were looking at a landskip, which we know are pregnant with meaning, but out of which we can never separate the meaning : for that reason, no doubt, commonly quoted (I think loosely) as instances of Dante's mysticism. They certainly, in a way we can hardly explain, concentrate into their imagery significances vital to the whole force of the poem : I mean, of course, such visions as the eagle in the Sixth Heaven, delineated by the incandescent souls of the just ; or the river of light,

> dipinte di mirabil primavera,

and the living jewels which issue from it and, for all their dazzling colour,

> son di lor vero umbriferi prefazii ;

217

and, above all, the White Rose made of the Blest :

> In forma dunque di candida rosa
> mi si mostrava la milizia santa
> che nel suo sangue Cristo fece sposa.

These are the things we can most easily refer to, if we are talking of Dante's characteristic eminence. Without these things, he could not be a great poet ; but neither could he be a great poet if these detachable things made up the whole account of his poetic achievement. And clearly not one of these things is present for its own sake in *The Divine Comedy ;* not one of them but is brought in by Dante most unmistakeably for the sake of something which transcends the sum of their separable virtues. Dante is obviously using them in the interest of his whole intention in the poem. Would it not therefore seem the natural thing, to go on with our account of Dante's achievement in the same way as we have begun, and from the organizing of language and imagery into characters, incidents, visions, to pass on to the organizing of these into Hell, Purgatory, Heaven, and so into the

Poetic Personality

divine method of continual justice ; and from this into the still closer unity, the living experience of the whole scheme of man's destiny as a thing personally seen and known, and thence to the very apex of the pyramid, the intense personality of Dante himself, the man who is capable of this experience ?

But it is just this continuation, this quite natural continuation, of poetic purpose, which recent criticism has declined to allow. The pyramid must be truncated ; there is a stage of its elevation at which poetry ceases to exist. I do not know why this stage should be placed at one point rather than another. It seems to me that if you once begin the poetic ascent you must, except by a quite arbitrary limitation, go on as far as it will take you ; and the poetic ascent has certainly begun when out of the meaning of words you allow a character, an incident, to form itself as poetry. But Croce and his followers decline to allow Dante any poetry except these momentary occurrences of it : and each moment occurs, they say, in its own right only : there is no continuity and accumulation of poetic effect in the series of the moments. Instead of allowing the obvious thing, that Dante is using each moment of his poem for the purpose of gradually establishing his whole intention ; this whole intention is regarded as a ready-made frame of carpentry into which poetic moments are fitted and let off like fireworks.

I doubt if theoretical ingenuity could be more surprisingly obtuse. Of course, when the poem is complete in our minds, we can see that it has a structure : but it is a structure which exists wholly by means of these moments, and has the same right to the name of poetry as they have. Suppose it true that the theme of *The Divine Comedy* is Catholic eschatology ; it is not half true and not a quarter true ; but if it was the whole truth, why should not this theme become poetry ? To expound an argument as such, is, no question of it, to fall from poetry. But if a poet gives us his vivid intuition of his argument and of all it means to him, if he expresses it as an experience, with a technique which can convey his exultation of reason, emotion, and spirit in living in the sense of truth,

and the labour and delight of attaining this, he is
giving us what must, by any workable definition,
be accepted as poetry. That is what Lucretius gives
us. And that, with much more completeness and
in a much more intricate harmony, is what *The
Divine Comedy* gives us : not the system of Catholic
theology, but the individual passion of experience
in which, by means of that system, a man feels he
understands and can love the inmost reality of things
and the purpose of the world. That is permanent,
however transitory the vehicle of it may be. Dante
lived in his theology like the electric current in a
metal wire. The energy was so intense that it
became radiant : and it is a conscious energy, and
sees the globe of its own illumination round about
it. He is living at the centre of spiritual reality ;
he becomes in his most personal quality the symbol
of man knowing and enjoying his destiny. And
there is absolutely no theoretical difference between
Dante's imaginary meeting with Farinata in Hell,
and his whole vision of Hell, Purgatory, and Heaven,
along with the sense of the order of divine justice
the vision implies. The one is as unmistakeably an

experience as the other. No one has ever ventured to question the superb poetic quality of the Farinata incident : and the criticism which denies the poetic quality of *The Divine Comedy* as a whole is simply criticism which is not capacious enough to contain it.

§ 3

Croce is a distinguisht authority ; but I have on my side an authority to whom I attribute greater importance—that of Dante himself : I mean Dante the constructive critic, the profound and meticulous theorist of poetry. He liked to hinge his principles on his own work : as he did in the *Convivio*, and the celebrated letter to Can Grande. And his main concern always was to show how a poem exists by reason of its whole intention ; it is the single result of the organization of all its detail, detail which exists for no other purpose than to combine in a single result. He would have been amused at the criticism which thinks it has done its duty in discriminating the quality of the detail in a work of art ; and he would have asked, in that formidable determination to get to the

Poetic Personality

bottom of things which we call *medieval*, how mere detail as such can give existence to a work of art at all.

Dante distinguishes two senses in a poem : what he calls the literal sense and the allegorical sense. On this hint, amazing and preposterous interpretations have been foisted into *The Divine Comedy*— interpretations which are allegorical in our sense of the word—political, philosophical, and what not. What Dante says himself is clear enough.[1] The literal sense of *The Divine Comedy* is the fortunes of certain souls after death. The allegorical sense is the destiny of man and the idea of perfect justice. " Allegorical " has come to be a somewhat misleading term. But assuredly it is true that there must be always two meanings in poetry, though there is, of course, no distinct line between them : " literal " will do as the name of the one, but the other we had better call " symbolic." A poet, we say, exists as a poet by expressing his experience. But whether this be an experience of everyday matter of fact, or a purely visionary experience as

[1] Letter to Can Grande (XIII, *Test. Crit.*).

223

strange and lofty as Dante's, one thing is certain : the experience itself will be incommunicable. The skill of the poet is to make, out of language and the effects of language, a reliable symbol of his experience ; and the symbol is understood, when the provocations of its imagery reverberate in emotions and allusions through our minds, in such a way that they finally collect themselves into an imaginary experience exactly corresponding to the original experience in the poet's mind.

But what impels a poet to express himself is the importance a thing has for him ; and that is nothing but the whole pattern of connexion and relation it has with other things—including, of course, the poet's own feelings. The poet is the man who sees in things an unusual degree of significance, an unusual complexity of fine and strong relationship with things far and near. Now Dante is the type of poet who finds nothing but this in the whole manner of his own life ; he is therefore typically the poet who is moved to express simply *himself* : not moods and moments of himself, but the whole scope and style of his personal experience, the whole stature and attitude of his personal existence. He had lived in experience as full and as varied as his time could offer ; and everything in it was a metaphor of all the rest. The most significant of all his experiences was so simply because it was the most intense, and because it came just when the characteristic habit of his life was beginning to establish itself. This was, of course, his early love for Beatrice. He spent the rest of his life celebrating it, for it became the centre round which everything else must organize itself. And it is easy to see why, with such a man as Dante. There was, raised to its highest power, all that we usually mean by the passion of love in this experience ; but also something which we do not usually expect to find in a love-affair. It had that significance for him which involves every faculty he can live in. Love, for Dante, could not but be an intellectual, as well as an emotional and a sensuous experience : his love of Beatrice saw in her not only the perfection of beauty but the perfection of understanding as well. It was, for him, impossible that the delight of the man who sees and feels could occur without

the illumination of the man who knows. He loves
Beatrice ; and that means that he understands the
world : or at least has seen himself understanding
the world. For to love her is to be aware of life's
perfection.

That Beatrice is the perfection of life is merely
confirmed in him by her early death : the angels
have petitioned for her presence in the only society
that is worthy of her. Henceforth she must live
on earth only in Dante's imagination. But this is
a life for her of continually increasing activity ; she
lives, that is, by being idealized : until nothing can
command his mind that is not a mode of her. And
so, when, after her death, he plunges himself in
philosophy for consolation, intellectual joys mean
the revived presence of Beatrice. As he could not
love her during her earthly life without a kindling
of intellect as well as of emotion, so now he cannot
have an intellectual ardor that does not recall the
image of her beauty.

But philosophy was not his only consolation. He
plunged also into fierce and gross passions, which
inspired some of the best of his early poetry. He

emerged bitterly repentant, rebuked by philosophy as an attribute of Beatrice, and by the vision of Beatrice with all the understanding of the world in her eyes. Yet it was only in idea that this hateful sin was punisht. He had turned traitor to what he knew was the best—to all that the image of Beatrice meant to him, to the service of the vision of perfection. He had proved faithless to this : and no actual punishment had followed. But also he had served most faithfully his country, as soldier and statesman ; and he knew the merits of his service. And what followed here ? Ignominy and disgrace. His wages were, to be a condemned man begging his way through exile. He had grievously sinned, and all the result was, a sense that he deserved punishment. He had done nobly, and the result was punishment that was bitterly real.

Henceforth he devotes himself to the vindication of the idea of justice. The more unjust these temporal realities are, the more triumphant becomes his belief in a justice ideal and eternal, making these bewildering moments of earthly life a necessary stage of its method. He recreates the affairs of this world under the evident law of an ultimate and unmistakeable justice, which lets nothing wrong go unpunisht, nothing good go unrewarded. He portrays Hell, Purgatory, Heaven ; and the whole range of life on the earth contributes to the vision. And over all his experience of this ideal world presides as his especial director—at first through a delegate and afterwards in person—the spirit of Beatrice, the image of the love which is also understanding—the image of that exalted experience which loves its own destiny because it can understand it. Need it be said, that Beatrice is Dante's image of his own profound desire ? Or that the theology of the poem is his symbol of the satisfaction of his desire ?

For this theological scheme of Hell, Purgatory, Heaven, and the superbly vivid substance in which it lives, is, of course, Dante's literal meaning in *The Divine Comedy*. If I had to stay there, the poem would be, for all the marvel of its verbal technique, a repellent curiosity. The literal meaning of *Inferno* is to me the most abominable superstition that has ever pestered humanity : pass from it to the religion of the Homeric Hymns, and you pass from barbarity into civilization.

But who ever thought of staying in the literal meaning of *The Divine Comedy*? No one, certainly, who reads it as poetry. Beyond, but by means of, this literal meaning, we see the symbolic meaning : we see the spirit of man placed in a world of implacable process, yet determined to create for itself its own sense of its destiny. And this, it has resolved, shall be in accordance with the most sublime faculty it has, the love of justice. Dante gives us this as it works itself out through the whole fate of man, and with a concentrated propriety of detail and lucidity of significance that make it more intensely our own than anything the actual world can offer. And at the climax of this story of eternal justice told in terms of earthly life, comes the vindication even of this. It is the nature of man to insist on justice : and we are made to feel that absolute reliance on justice will at last bring man's mind into perfect accord with the unspeakable inmost reality of things. We live, therefore, the whole possibility of this world in one great coherence.

The Idea of Great Poetry

From the depths of lewd and detestable crime up to the height of indescribable ecstasy, the whole conceivable range of human faculty—rebellion and submission, torment and delight—becomes a single harmony of impression, when Hell, Purgatory, and Heaven have finally organized their sequence.

That is the very thing we have found to be required for greatness in poetry. But for the supremely great, something more than this, we found, was needed : namely, the concentration of this in a figure of vividly personal life. And here is the acme of the symbolic meaning of *The Divine Comedy*. The figure of Dante himself is the immortal, unchangeable thing that steps out of his poem : the intensely individual figure, with all its resentments and abasements, indignations and pities, its pride and its love, its generous glorying in the good and ferocious scorn of the evil. Symbolic personality is, from the very nature of the poem's form, the thing which *The Divine Comedy* gives us more remarkably than any other poem. For the whole process of events in the poem is the process of the spiritual experience of Dante himself : and out of it all emerges the personal man, who takes on himself the demand that destiny shall be just, and satisfies the demand by *understanding* the act of destiny as the act of justice. Dante is not only the type of the grand style in poetry, but of the grand style in man's commerce with his destiny.

Let me, in conclusion, just say that the instances of great poetry which I have given you have not been meant to represent anything like a complete series. I have said nothing of Sophocles or Pindar or Virgil, Tasso or Calderon or Racine. I have made but trifling references to Chaucer, to Æschylus, and other poets only less important than these. But I merely brought those poets in who would, I thought, make my argument clear. If they have not done that, they have at least, I hope, directed your thoughts to an aspect of poetry which, it seems to me, needs some emphasis to-day. I do not mean merely the quality of greatness ; but that which makes the quality of greatness possible. I have indicated it often enough, and perhaps too often, by the distinction between *poetry* and *poems*.

The Idea of Great Poetry

*Form—coherence—unity—*these are well-worn terms ; and just because they are, I thought it a fitting topic for such a course as this to argue in favour of their unchangeable importance, by considering poems which cannot rightly be appreciated at all, unless these terms have some meaning for us.